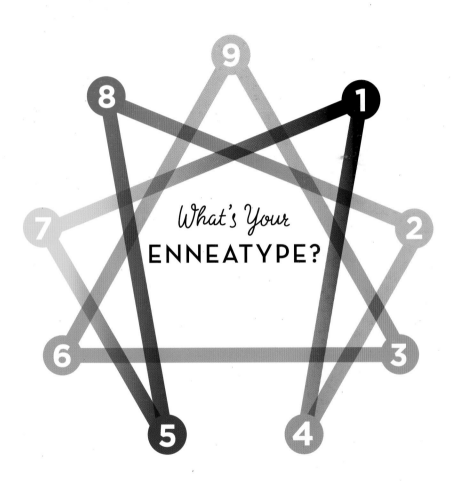

What's Your

ENNEATYPE?

Inspiring | Educating | Creating | Entertaining

Brimming with creative inspiration, how-to projects, and useful information to enrich your everyday life, Quarto Knows is a favorite destination for those pursuing their interests and passions. Visit our site and dig deeper with our books into your area of interest: Quarto Creates, Quarto Cooks, Quarto Homes, Quarto Lives, Quarto Drives, Quarto Explores, Quarto Gifts, or Quarto Kids.

First Published in 2020 by Fair Winds Press, an imprint of The Quarto Group,
100 Cummings Center, Suite 265-D, Beverly, MA 01915, USA.
T (978) 282-9590 F (978) 283-2742 QuartoKnows.com

TO THE BRAIN TRUST,

THIS IS ONLY BECAUSE OF YOU,

AND THESE ARE YOUR WORDS

AS MUCH AS THEY ARE OURS.

Fair Winds Press titles are also available at discount for retail, wholesale, promotional, and bulk purchase. For details, contact the Special Sales Manager by email at specialsales@quarto.com or by mail at The Quarto Group, Attn: Special Sales Manager, 100 Cummings Center, Suite 265-D, Beverly, MA 01915, USA.

24 23 22 21 20   2 3 4 5

ISBN: 978-1-59233-952-5

Digital edition published in 2020
eISBN: 978-1-63159-885-2

Library of Congress Cataloging-in-Publication Data

Names: Carver, Liz, author. | Green, Josh (Psychologist), author.
Title: What's your enneatype? : an essential guide to the enneagram :
    understanding the nine personality types for personal growth and
    strengthened relationships / Liz Carver, Josh Green.
Description: Beverly : Fair Winds Press, 2020. | Includes index.
Identifiers: LCCN 2020005263 | ISBN 9781592339525 (trade paperback) | ISBN 9781631598852 (ebook)
Subjects: LCSH: Typology (Psychology) | Enneagram. | Self-actualization
    (Psychology)
Classification: LCC BF698.3 .C378 2020 | DDC 155.2/6—dc23
LC record available at https://lccn.loc.gov/2020005263

Interior Design and Page Layout: Laura Klynstra

Printed in China

What's Your
ENNEATYPE?

● ● ● ● ● ● ● ● ●

Understanding the Nine Personality

Types for Personal Growth and

Strengthened Relationships

● ● ● ● ● ● ● ● ●

LIZ CARVER AND JOSH GREEN

FAIR WINDS

1 2 3

4 5 6

7 8 9

CONTENTS

● ● ● ● ● ● ● ● ● ●

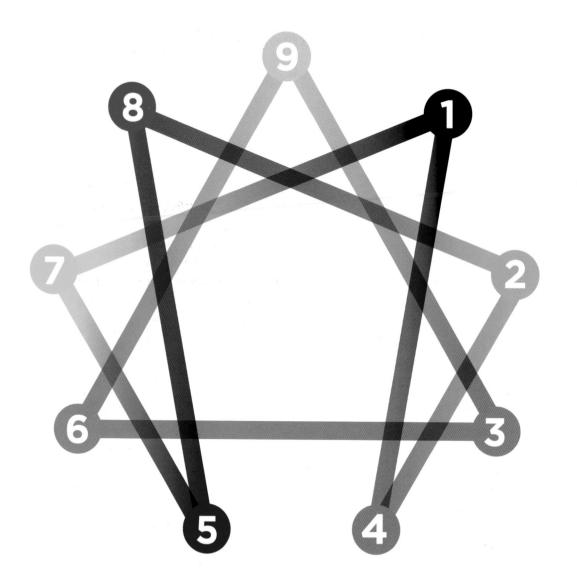

THE ENNEAGRAM:
What It Is and What It Isn't

• • • • • • • • •

Imagine your ideal dinner party. Who is there? Where is it? When is it? Are you hosting or cooking? Who helps you? Who is invited? Engage your senses. What does it look like? Sound like? Smell like? What will you eat? How and when does it end?

No matter what your answer is to those questions, it reveals a lot about you. Liz likes to host dinner parties in her home for small groups of invited guests. She makes way too much food in advance of the guests arriving, and they casually eat, drink, talk about everything, and listen to records until she eventually kicks everyone out by ten o'clock. She doesn't like her guests to do any work, and she always want to eat on beautiful dishes that are themed to the occasion. She creates a lot of structure and does a lot of work so that there can be as much freedom and relaxation in the middle as possible. Josh, on the other hand, wouldn't be hosting in his ideal dinner party scenario; rather, the party would be at one of his best friend's homes. This way the friend can be in charge of details, but Josh can be the number-one copilot and sous chef, making or preparing whatever it is that's needed. He would be among the first people there and the last one to leave. He could float around the room and have all sorts of fun conversations with a variety of people. The party would last for hours and hours, and the night would end with some sort of deep conversation with whoever was willing to stick it out.

We like this dinner party exercise because it reminds us just how differently each person is wired. Every response to this question is revealing. Whether you want to host, like Liz, or be the social butterfly, like Josh (or maybe you don't even want to go to a dinner party), every response reveals something about the person answering it.

We all see the world through a unique set of lenses that have been crafted over time. Our genetics, predispositions, families of origin, personalities, experiences, traumas, ages, socioeconomic status, ethnicities, and cultures all contribute to the way that we see the world and the way that we operate within it. Throughout life, we learn how to show up in the world, and by the time we're in our twenties, barring any unexpected trauma, we have pretty nearly landed on a way of operating. The problem is that not all of the ways that we have learned to operate are good, helpful, or healthy. Many of our habits are actually coping mechanisms we learned early on, many of our lenses are clouded by childhood wounds, and many of our reactions in the world are formed by unhealthy patterns.

The Enneagram is a tool that helps us name what motivates people to do the things they do in the world. It is not a personality test, but rather a framework to be learned. In other words, it does not aim to help us understand *what* people do but *why* they do what they do. More than anything, the Enneagram invites you to grow out of how you've been operating, unlearn bad habits, and rewrite unhealthy narratives.

What It Is

NINE-POINTED FIGURE

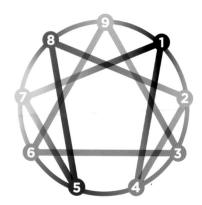

The Enneagram is many things. The word itself means "nine-pointed figure," and the figure is an incredibly helpful teaching tool. Each of the nine spokes represents a different type ("Enneatype"), named from "ONE" through "NINE" (simply generic words used to describe these types). Type NINE is on the top middle, and numbers ONE through EIGHT move around clockwise.

Each type is connected to two other types by lines that intersect the diagram. These lines, which we will describe in greater detail later on, depict the movements of *integration* (growth, health, wellness) and *disintegration* (stress, unhealth, chaos) for each type. Built into the Enneagram figure itself is the understanding that we are not always our best selves. Sometimes we are operating on empty and are unable to show up in the world in the way we would like to (disintegration). In these movements of disintegration, we take on some of the unhealthiest characteristics of the type to which we disintegrate, which is depicted by these connecting lines. Other times, we are the best version of ourselves and are able to transcend our daily behaviors to be something even greater (integration). In these movements of integration, we take on some of the healthiest characteristics of the type to which we integrate, depicted by the line connecting both types.

Sometimes the Enneagram is drawn with a circle around the outside (see illustration above). This depiction now has four connecting lines from each type to another, the lines of integration and disintegration we already discussed and lines around the outside that connect each type to its adjacent numbers. These lines depict wings, the two types adjacent to your core type whose characteristics may influence the way you show up in the world. You may find that you have one wing, both (balanced) wings, or no wing at all. You will continue to see the Enneagram as a nine-pointed figure to help you remember about the interconnectedness of all nine types.

A TOOL FOR PERSONAL GROWTH

First and foremost, the Enneagram is a tool for personal growth. The Enneagram is not necessarily focused on what you do. Rather, it gets to the core of why you do what you do and provides an invitation for you to start to unlearn your bad habits, rewrite your unhealthy narratives, and grow into a more integrated you.

We love personality systems. At different times in our lives, we have both geeked out on the Myers-Briggs Type Indicator (MBTI). (Josh is an ESFJ and Liz is an INTJ.) But at a certain point, we found ourselves looking for more. Liz found that some of the sharp edges described in her INTJ-ness weren't as true as they used to be. While she still valued and referenced the MBTI system, it was only offering her self-knowledge. What she was really looking for was formation and growth. Enter the Enneagram, which demands you understand that self-knowledge is not an end in itself, but rather an invitation to grow.

A TOOL TO CHALLENGE YOU

There can be no growth without change, and change is inherently painful. Enneagram teacher Richard Rohr writes, "Self-knowledge is tied in with inner work, which is both demanding and painful." What this means is that the Enneagram, and even this very book, is going to challenge you.

At the beginning of each chapter, you will see a large numerical icon for each type with a long shadow cast by it. This is to depict that while each of these nine types are centered on a motivation, they are also centered on a shadow side. We encourage you to be truthful with yourself as you read this book. Each type has a very dark shadow side, and that shadow side is what we need to root out, relearn, and grow beyond. One of the points of the Enneagram is to learn about how the best and worst of you are very much related. We need to know our flaws and our unhealthy motivations if we want to rise above them and become more integrated and healthy people.

We frequently receive messages and comments from people on our Instagram account (@justmyenneatype) complaining about how they "got the worst type" or how we are "always so mean" to their type. There is no worst or best type, and we work hard to be consistent, fair, and objective in how we talk about all nine types. When we receive these messages, we usually know what's going on under the surface for this person: The truth of the Enneagram has hit a chord with their shadow side, and that discomfort is painful and challenging.

Take those moments of discomfort and do something with them. They are gifts to you, inviting you to grow and heal.

A MASTER CLASS IN EMPATHY

The Enneagram is also a tool that helps us understand other people. By reading this book, you will learn about nine very different ways that people around you see the world. It's a good reminder that not everyone thinks the way that you think. Just because someone has similar external characteristics or reactions to you doesn't mean that they are doing what they are doing for the same reason.

We work with many people of different ethnicities, countries of origin, socioeconomic statuses, generations, religions, orientations, and more. We both also work for organizations that deeply value diversity. To work in a diverse community means that you will inevitably encounter friction—maybe even daily. Understanding the Enneagram and how those around us are wired helps us better understand why someone may be reacting harshly, lashing out, or shutting down and withdrawing; why certain work teams are dysfunctional; or why other teams work very well. The Enneagram unlocks another layer of diversity and calls us to empathize with others. As you learn about these nine types, we hope you will find that your compassion and empathy for others around you will grow.

What It Isn't

NOT A PARTY TRICK

The Enneagram is a tool that you can use for good or for bad. One of the recent ways that people have been abusing the Enneagram, due to its extreme rise in popularity, is as a party trick of sorts, a way to "reveal" information about people that "shows off" their secret knowledge about other people.

So let's get it straightened out. First and foremost, this is a tool for you. It is a tool for you to use in your own personal growth and a tool that will likely help you grow and heal your relationships as you begin to understand those around you. This is not a tool for you to use to label other people or to trivialize as some sort of game. Doing so minimizes people to their externalized actions and to your own perception of who they are, and it puts them in a box. This is hurtful behavior, and we have heard from hundreds of people in our online community who don't want to share their Enneatypes for this very reason.

NOT AN EXCUSE

A common critique of the Enneagram is that when people first learn about it, they stop at self-knowledge. As stated before, the Enneagram demands that you understand that self-knowledge is not an end in itself; it is an invitation to grow. For example, a TWO who learns they are a TWO doesn't get to use TWO-ness as an excuse to be prideful. Pride is the shadow side of TWO and needs to be rooted out.

As a result, many people are very turned off from the Enneagram because they are not ready or unable to face their shadow sides. That is okay—don't pressure them. The Enneagram is for you to do your work, not for you to do other people's work.

NOT JUST NINE TYPES

On one level, yes, there are only nine base archetypes built into the Enneagram. But there is so much more built in. The lines of the Enneagram figure that we described earlier (see page 8) show how each type changes depending on their health (integration/disintegration). Each type can also have a wing that shades and informs how they show up as their type. There are also three instinctual subtypes to each type that add even greater depth. To give an example, one EIGHT could be actually a Social Instinct EIGHT with a SEVEN wing, which would be a vastly different sort of EIGHT than a Self-Preservation Instinct EIGHT with a NINE wing.

Take a quick look back at the cover of this book. You will see the nine types running across the top in solid colors. But bleeding from each color is a range of shades of that color. So, going back to our example, if EIGHTs are red, it's important to remember that there are many shades of red, just as there are many different types of EIGHTs. All that being said, the Enneagram, while incredibly helpful, will never tell you everything about who you are.

How to Figure Out Your Enneatype

The best way to discover your Enneatype is by learning about all nine types. A good practice is to write numbers one through nine on a piece of paper and, as you learn about each type, cross off the types that you are definitely not. Many people will be left with their type in the end, and some will have an aha moment with their type as soon as they encounter it.

It's important to remember that the Enneagram is not a test; it is a framework of understanding. This isn't quantitative work we're doing; it's qualitative. Good results will take more time, and that's part of the journey. At best, Enneagram tests will point you in the right direction but never confirm your type. Only you can do that. Even then, they're only helpful if you are self-aware enough to answer them accurately.

You can really only find your Enneatype by reading, researching, and learning. As you get to the core needs, fears, and motivations, one of them will likely become clear to you. Some people know their type in three minutes, while other people will take years to figure it out. Both of these—and anywhere in between—are all very normal.

If you find yourself torn between two or three different types, pay attention to growth and stress numbers. Pay special attention to the core fears, needs, and motivations, and dig deeper into subtypes. But, most importantly, pay attention to what makes you uncomfortable about those types and see what resonates with you. Oftentimes the type that makes you the most uncomfortable is resonating with your shadow side and might be telling you something about which type you are.

How to Read This Book

We wrote this book to be a resource to you. We believe the Enneagram can help you grow, and we hope that this book will be fun to look at but will also open up doorways for healing and growth in your life and relationships.

Don't feel any pressure to read the nine types in any particular order. You can start with ONE or start with NINE and read backwards. Start with your own type (if you know it!) and jump around; it's your book. Here are just a few terms that you will encounter in each chapter that might be helpful to come back to as you read:

SUBTYPES

One part of the Enneagram that unlocks a lot of clarity is the nature of subtypes, or instincts. Each person is dominant in one of three instincts: Social (SO), Sexual (SX), or Self-Preservation (SP). That instinct within your type is your subtype. Each person also has a secondary subtype and will likely find that one of the three instincts does not relate to them. For example, a NINE could be a SO/SX NINE, meaning their dominant subtype is Social and their secondary subtype is Sexual.

»⟶ Social (SO) types find their place in a group, seek personal connection, and act with the interest of the group in mind. As you read each chapter, you will find a description of how the Social Instinct manifests itself for that particular type.

»⟶ Sexual (SX) types, sometimes called Intimate or One-to-One types, are motivated by finding the stimulation of connecting with other people. Sexual types are often more intense and openly passionate than the other instincts. As you read each chapter, you will find a description of how the Sexual Instinct manifests itself for that particular type.

»⟶ Self-Preservation (SP) types are motivated by protecting themselves from the world around them in very tangible ways. This is primarily how they find their safety and security. As you read each chapter, you will find a description of how the Self-Preservation Instinct manifests itself for that particular type.

»⟶ *Countertype* is a word you will encounter in each chapter as you read about subtypes. Countertypes may have a difficult time discovering their type, as they go against the grain of their core type. A countertype for NINE, for example, will show up in the world as a less NINE-ish NINE while still internally experiencing all of the motivations, core fears, needs, and gifts a NINE does.

WINGS

Wings are the two types adjacent to a central type whose characteristics you can take on to varying degrees. Some people have a very strong wing, some people have a very slight wing, some people are balanced between both wings, and some people have no wing at all. The syntax we use to describe a wing is with the letter *w* between two numbers. So, a THREE who has a FOUR wing would be a 3w4.

TRIADS

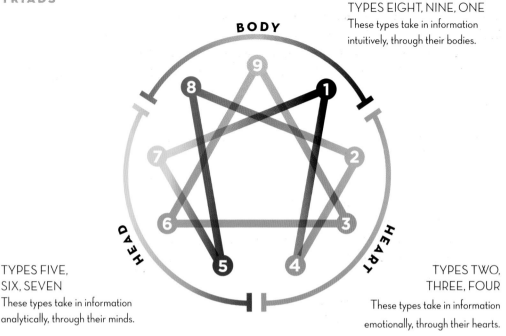

BODY

TYPES EIGHT, NINE, ONE
These types take in information
intuitively, through their bodies.

TYPES FIVE,
SIX, SEVEN
These types take in information
analytically, through their minds.

TYPES TWO,
THREE, FOUR
These types take in information
emotionally, through their hearts.

The Enneagram is divided into three triads: Body, Head, and Heart. The triads explain to us how we take in information, as well as our relationships to anger, fear, and shame.

»—→ All three types in the **Heart Triad** (TWO, THREE, and FOUR) take in information emotionally, through their feelings. They have feelings about everything they encounter. While every type has feelings, unless you are in the Heart Triad, body awareness or thinking will come first as you take in information, even if it is only for a split second. These types are tuned into and experience themselves in relation to the feelings or behaviors of others. Also called the Shame Triad, all three of these types struggle with feelings of worthlessness.

»—→ All three types in the **Head Triad** (FIVE, SIX, and SEVEN) take in information analytically, through their minds. While every type has thoughts about everything, unless you are in the Head Triad, body awareness or feelings will come first as you take in information, even if it is only for a split second. They are observational people who depend on fact and logic rather than feelings or emotions. Also called the Fear Triad, all three of these types have difficulty making decisions and planning for the future.

»→ All three types in the **Body Triad** (EIGHT, NINE, and ONE) take in information intuitively, through their bodies. When they walk into a room, they have gut feelings about what needs to be done, even before they have a thought or emotional response to their environment. All three of the types in the Body Triad wrestle with a desire for things to be set right. Also called the Anger Triad, all three of these types wrestle with anger.

STANCES

The Enneagram also consists of three stances. The Dependent Stance, the Withdrawing Stance, and the Aggressive Stance, have a lot to do with our general approach toward other people and toward time.

»→ ONEs, TWOs, and SIXes are a part of the **Dependent Stance,** meaning that they are oriented toward others and their sense of identity comes from their relationships. They are community minded, seeking reassurance from other people. Unsurprisingly, these types can struggle with thinking for themselves in a productive manner. As such, the Dependent Stance is often referred to as "thinking-repressed." This does not mean that ONEs, TWOs, and SIXes do not think, but rather that their thinking is less productive than other types. All three Dependent Stance types believe that they must earn the right to have their needs met.

STANCES

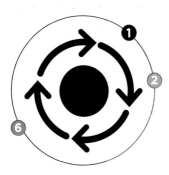 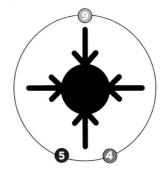 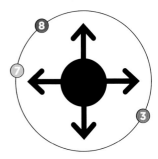

DEPENDENT
TYPES ONE, TWO, SIX

These types are oriented towards others, and their sense of self comes from outside of themselves. They are community minded and seek reassurance from other people.

WITHDRAWING
TYPES FOUR, FIVE, NINE

These types are oriented inwards, and their sense of self comes from within. They meet their own needs internally and make decisions in the privacy of their own hearts and minds.

AGGRESSIVE
TYPES THREE, SEVEN, EIGHT

These types are oriented outwards against others, have a strong sense of self, and are assertive or aggressive in naming their needs and what they want.

What's Your Enneatype?

»—→ FOURs, FIVEs, and NINEs are part of the **Withdrawing Stance**, meaning that they are oriented inward and their identity and sense of self come from within. These types meet their own needs internally and make decisions in the privacy of their own minds and hearts. The Withdrawing Stance is often referred to as "doing-repressed." This does not mean that FOURs, FIVEs, and NINEs do not "do," but rather that their doing is less productive than other types. They may have difficulty moving their ideas to completion. All three types in the Withdrawing Stance are more oriented toward the past than other types, largely because no "doing" is needed in the past. They may replay conversations and scenarios over many times in their heads, thinking about what they should have done or said differently.

»—→ THREEs, SEVENs, and EIGHTs are a part of the **Aggressive Stance**, meaning that they are oriented outward against others and are assertive (or aggressive) in naming their needs and seeing them met. They know what they want, they know where they want to go, and they will go there, not allowing things or people to stand in their way. All three Aggressive Stance types are oriented toward the future rather than the present or past, believing nothing will happen in the future unless they make it happen. All three Aggressive Stance types may also find it hard to fully get in touch with their own feelings, leading some to use the term "feeling-repressed" when talking about THREEs, SEVENs, and EIGHTS. This can be better understood by saying that these three types do and think more than they feel. These types are more dismissive of feelings in general. Feelings are not readily available in their own lives, so they may struggle to make space for the feelings of others, not because they are intentionally being dismissive, but merely because feelings are not on their radar.

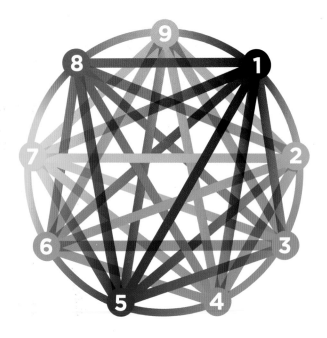

MISSED CONNECTIONS

We believe that, at the end of the day, people are all more similar than dissimilar. While the Enneagram as it's traditionally drawn only has lines that connect the nine types in their movements of integration and disintegration, we have experienced that all nine types are connected in more complex ways. Therefore, in each chapter, we include a section that explains what we call the "Missed Connections" for that type. These are the ways in which two types not traditionally linked together will find crossover and resonance.

THE RECKONING

"The Reckoning" may sound harsh, but after studying the Enneagram for some time, we began to notice a marked difference between people of the same type. Some people had been through a life event, trauma, or situation that had tenderized them greatly to the point that they were a very different sort of person on the other side. These events didn't seem to be connected to age or maturity insomuch as they were paradigmatic shifts that cut the person down enough to the point where they could no longer go on autopilot and depend on the coping mechanisms of their type. As a result of this finding, we informally started to refer to this paradigm shift as the Reckoning. In each chapter, we include a section that explains what the Reckoning will likely look like for each type—what sort of paradigm shift may be necessary for that type to snap out of their cycle and really have a true wake-up call.

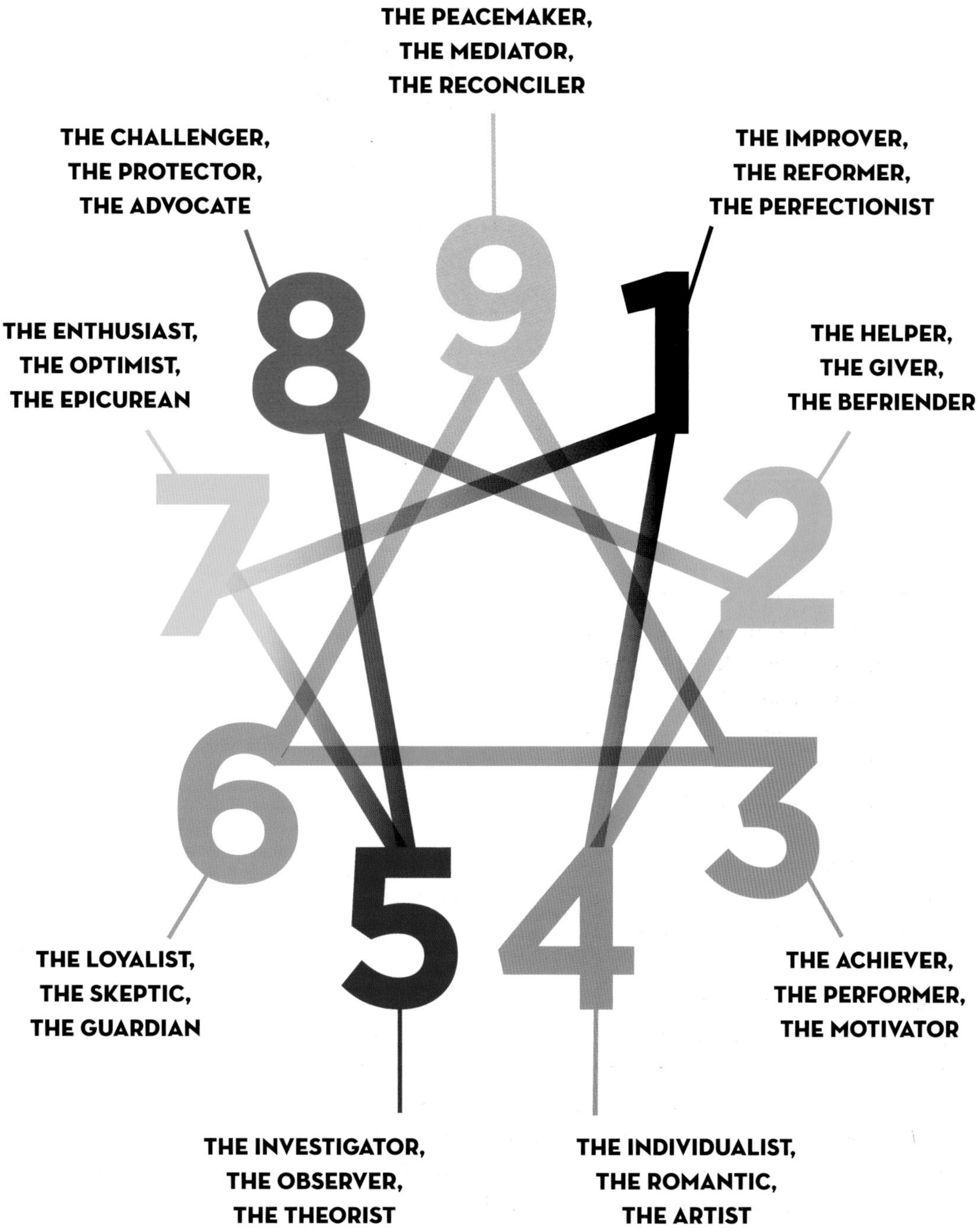

THE PEACEMAKER,
THE MEDIATOR,
THE RECONCILER

THE CHALLENGER,
THE PROTECTOR,
THE ADVOCATE

THE IMPROVER,
THE REFORMER,
THE PERFECTIONIST

THE ENTHUSIAST,
THE OPTIMIST,
THE EPICUREAN

THE HELPER,
THE GIVER,
THE BEFRIENDER

8 9 1

7 2

6 3

5 4

THE LOYALIST,
THE SKEPTIC,
THE GUARDIAN

THE ACHIEVER,
THE PERFORMER,
THE MOTIVATOR

THE INVESTIGATOR,
THE OBSERVER,
THE THEORIST

THE INDIVIDUALIST,
THE ROMANTIC,
THE ARTIST

THE IMPROVER, THE REFORMER, THE PERFECTIONIST

Life Strategy: "I must be perfect and do what is right."

Needs to: make things right/better

Actions are motivated by: integrity, balance, ethics, fear of condemnation, fear of being bad, anger, avoiding blame, correcting mistakes

Shadow Side: often struggle with an Inner Critic, a relentless condemning inner voice

THE HELPER, THE GIVER, THE BEFRIENDER

Life Strategy: "I must be helpful, caring, and needed."

Needs to: be needed

Actions are motivated by: fear or isolation, shame of not being needed by others, fear of disconnection

Shadow Side: often struggle to know who they are

THE ACHIEVER, THE PERFORMER, THE MOTIVATOR

Life Strategy: "I must be impressive and look accomplished and successful."

Needs to: be successful/seen as successful

Actions are motivated by: desire to be admired, successful, valuable, respected

Shadow Side: often so afraid of failing that they may struggle with honesty with themselves/others

THE INDIVIDUALIST, THE ROMANTIC, THE ARTIST

Life Strategy: "I must be understood uniquely as I am."

Needs to: be different, creative, stand out, find their voice

Actions are motivated by: desire to be authentic, to be their unique self, to express themselves to the world, to make the world a more beautiful place

Shadow Side: burdened by the shame of feeling more broken than others

THE INVESTIGATOR, THE OBSERVER, THE THEORIST

Life Strategy: "I must be knowledgeable and equipped."

Needs to: understand, comprehend, know

Actions are motivated by: desire to be capable and competent, to explore reality, to remain undisturbed by others, to be independent

Shadow Side: terrified of invasion by others and of ignorance and emptiness

THE LOYALIST, THE SKEPTIC, THE GUARDIAN

Life Strategy: "I must be secure/safe."

Needs to: be safe, survive, plan for the worst

Actions are motivated by: desire for security and guidance, to have the support of others, to protect, to feel certain, to care for others

Shadow Side: often can be paralyzed by fear and anxiety from the potential worst-case scenario

THE ENTHUSIAST, THE OPTIMIST, THE EPICUREAN

Life Strategy: "I must be enjoying myself and avoiding pain."

Needs to: have fun/new experiences

Actions are motivated by: desire to be happy, to enjoy life, to keep options open, to have fun!

Shadow Side: often their fun nature masks an inability to experience pain and suffering

THE CHALLENGER, THE PROTECTOR, THE ADVOCATE

Life Strategy: "I must be strong and outside the control of others."

Needs to: never be controlled by anyone

Actions are motivated by: desire to be self-reliant, to be truthful, to seek justice for all

Shadow Side: often struggle with the fear of being controlled

THE PEACEMAKER, THE MEDIATOR, THE RECONCILER

Life Strategy: "I must maintain peace and calm."

Needs to: find peace at any cost

Actions are motivated by: desire to have peace of mind, to create harmony in their environment, and to avoid conflict/tension

Shadow Side: struggle with sense of self due to constant peace-keeping

What's Your Enneatype?

ABOUT THE COLORS

Finally, a note on the colors. We use one unique color for each type, and these colors were not chosen at random. Here is some more information on each color and why we chose it:

»→ **The colors for ONEs are black and white.** ONEs see the world in black and white— there is no ambiguity in how they see anything. ONEs are known to have a clear sense of right and wrong. Black and white are clean, precise colors, similar to how ONEs see the world in a logical, orderly way. Black is a solid, strong, and consistent color. You can never go wrong wearing a black suit or a black dress. This is similar to how healthy ONEs embody consistency and decisiveness in a way that most other types do not.

»→ **The color for TWOs is blue.** In nature, blue is most commonly associated with the sky and the sea, which represents TWOs in several ways. Calm waters and clear blue skies demonstrate calmness, peace, and stability, which are qualities that TWOs can embody. The sky and sea can also bring about fierce storms, which is appropriate because TWOs can love like a "mighty ocean," as the artist Sleeping at Last describes in the song "Two," moving mountains to give the love needed to the people in their lives. However, like a force of nature, TWOs can also disrupt everyone else's apparent peace and calmness if they feel unappreciated or taken advantage of for too long, bringing out a more chaotic storm.

»→ **The color for THREEs is orange.** THREEs are known to be engaging and winsome, so the vibrancy of orange captures the way that many people are drawn to THREEs. Orange is also associated with health and vitality (think fruits and vitamin C), which speaks to the productivity and efficiency of THREEs. Finally, while THREEs are known to have strong, confident personalities, they are also known to constantly adapt to their environment so that they can be seen as successful, however that may look in any given situation. Thus, THREEs are represented by a secondary color that, while bright and strong, is not a primary color all by itself.

»→ **The color for FOURs is purple.** Purple is one of the rarest naturally occurring colors, which is perfect for our unique FOUR friends who love to be known and understood as individuals. Purple is a secondary color, a mixture of the coolness of blue and vibrancy of red. Purple itself can be used both as a cool color and a warm color, which is similar to how FOURs can experience the dramatic oscillation of deep "hot and cold" feelings all the time. In the ancient Near East, purple represented wealth and royalty and was saved for only the finest of clothes and other goods. It is the unicorn of colors, and FOURs are the unicorn of types.

The color for FIVEs is green. FIVEs are observant and prone to take in information with their eyes, and eyes can recognize more shades of green than any other color. Green is also the most restful color for human eyes to view, and many schools and institutions are painted green to calm nerves and anxieties. FIVEs tend to run out of energy, so a restful color caters to their need to recharge. Green is often used to bring balance to the primary colors when they are being used in a way that is either too warm or too cool, which speaks to the objectivity and non-dualism that FIVEs embody.

The color for SIXes is brown. Brown is one of two neutral colors. Neutral should not be read as "boring," because SIXes are anything *but* bland. There is quite a variety of browns in the world, from bronze to coffee to mahogany to chestnut to khaki to sand. Look at the subtypes and you will see that out of all of the numbers, SIXes have the most variety among the three different instincts. The very ground that supports us, both indoors and outdoors, is often brown, not unlike how SIXes in health provide support and stability for the people in their lives. Brown is not a loud, vibrant color; rather, it is adaptable and goes with any environment.

The color for SEVENs is yellow. The line "The sun will come out tomorrow" was probably written by a SEVEN. It's only fitting that the color associated with bright, sunny days is the color of our optimistic, enthusiastic SEVEN friends. Yellow is warm and vibrant, characteristics attributed to SEVENs. SEVENs embody the sun that comes after the storm with persistent optimism. They are assertive people with a strong sense of self, so a primary color is fitting for them. They are often very high-energy people, so such a vibrant color could capture these classic SEVEN traits.

The color for EIGHTs is red. Think of some of the stereotypes associated with red. It's supposed to make bulls angry. Red cars allegedly get the most speeding tickets. Red lights and stop signs seem to yell "NO!" at you. All of these point to the loudness and intensity with which our strong, assertive EIGHT friends often live their lives. Red is a primary color, which is representative of how EIGHTs have a more confident sense of self than most other types. Red can also be associated with passion, and EIGHTs love when their intensity is met with an equal intensity, rather than backing down in fear.

»—→ The color for NINEs is gray. Gray is a combination of black and white. A classic trait of NINEs is how they can relate to and empathize with both sides in any situation. While some of the other types have very strong senses of self, NINEs have a very vague sense of self, so a blurrier, less vibrant color fits them. NINEs sometimes struggle to know what they actually want or need in any situation because they merge with other people, subconsciously deleting themselves from the equation. As a result, they can be very content, go-with-the-flow types of people, so it's only appropriate for them to be a neutral color like gray that can go with anything.

So there you have it. We are excited for you to dig into this book and learn more about the Enneagram. We hope you learn more about yourself and the people around you. But more than that, we hope you accept the invitation that the Enneagram offers you: to deal with your shadow self and grow out of how you've been operating. We hope you name and unlearn bad habits and rewrite unhealthy narratives.

We hope you enjoy this book as much as we enjoyed writing it. Thank you for trusting us with your time. Welcome to your journey with the Enneagram.

—Josh and Liz

T Y P E

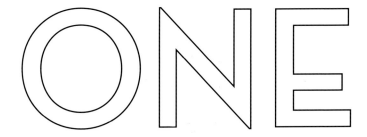

The Improver / Reformer / Perfectionist

Enneagram ONEs

Enneagram ONEs are the improvers and reformers of the world. They are focused, hardworking, precise, detail-oriented people who operate from a strong sense of personal ethics. They have a very specific sense of what is right and what is wrong in any and all situations, and they will work themselves to exhaustion to make sure that right wins in the end.

ONEs are bold and courageous, living lives of great conviction. They are willing to take a stand for what is right, are willing to sacrifice themselves for what is right, and—best of all—they intuitively *know* what is right. Some ONEs are perfectionistic, but all are principled, focused, and critical. They carry a heavy load on their backs, weighed down by a strong sense of personal integrity, a sense of responsibility, and a focus on a higher purpose.

ONEs love people deeply, and they are sensitive of others. Much of their senses of fairness, objectivity, and ethics are rooted in their love for others. They want the world to be a better place for everyone. They feel a deep sense of responsibility to their people and will work themselves to death to fulfill their responsibilities and improve the world.

While it seems that ONEs live much of their lives in their heads, it may be surprising to learn that their minds are not necessarily a safe space. Unlike other types, ONEs are burdened by something called an "Inner Critic." It can be shocking for ONEs to hear that not everyone has a critical voice in their head. This inner voice is harsh, relentless, punishing, and constantly monitoring the ONE's every thought, word, or deed as it judges everything they think and do.

In our work with the Enneagram, we have yet to find a ONE who does not have an Inner Critic or someone of any other type who has an Inner Critic. ONEs describe their Inner Critics as relentless, conniving, loud, shaming, abusive, harsh, and cruel. We asked our ONE friend, Hil, to describe what her Inner Critic sounds like, and here is what she said via email:

" My inner critic is male. He's conniving, exasperated, spitting mad, and a catastrophizing instigator. He's rarely quiet.

His favorite tool is shame. He says things like, "Look at what you did, that was so messed up, you'll never amount to anything." On bad days, he says those things once every few seconds through a megaphone. On good days, he's there but in the background, like I realized he's pitiful and finally put him in a corner to mutter to himself. Most days, he's a little muffled and running like the stock market banner at the bottom of a news screen. Abusive, but I know he's a sham.

I could get a lot more done and believe in myself a whole lot more if there wasn't a constant question mark on everything I say, think, do, and feel. "

1

To those of you reading this book who are not ONEs, we hope these words fill you with empathy and compassion for your ONE friends living with a critical voice like this in their heads. For those of you who are ONEs or perhaps realizing you are a ONE for the first time because of Hil's words, we want to encourage you to keep naming when your Inner Critic speaks to you and what she or he says. Your Inner Critic is more than just your own conscience. Your Inner Critic is not the voice of God, and it is not a voice that you need to listen to or even entertain. We hope to give you some practical and concrete ways to silence your Inner Critic in this chapter.

To the ONE reading this right now, remind yourself that this chapter is not criticism of your soul: It is an invitation to grow. Type ONEs, more than any other type, reflect the goodness and rightness of the world, and we live in a world that desperately needs to see what rightness and goodness really look like. Be encouraged as you read.

A World of ONEs

The world would have the potential to be an orderly, systematized place where justice prevails. However, in a world full of people with good intentions and Inner Critics with different definitions of right and good, chaos would ensue. Everyone would have their own idea of what is right, and nothing would get done. There would be great potential for peace, due to the focus on morality, and a great probability of stress because of the focus on perfectionism. At its worst, the world would become like a dystopian novel, where order robs the world of humanity. At its best, the world would be a tidy, ethical utopia filled with hardworking, exhausted, well-meaning perfectionists.

Motivation

A ONE's motivation has to do with right and wrong. They want to have integrity and be ethical. They want to correct mistakes, avoid blame and criticism, and even be beyond criticism. They want to be "good," so they are constantly improving themselves, others, and the world. They may fear condemnation and criticism so deeply that they overwork, overthink, and strive to be beyond condemnation. Some ONEs may even feel an addiction to perfection.

Anger is a huge motivator for ONEs, though they may not be able to admit this easily. For some ONEs, to even admit that they have a well of anger and resentment inside themselves would mean to admit that they are not as good as they think they are or as good as they think they ought to be. This is because ONEs are afraid of being bad, evil, or wrong, of being deemed irresponsible or inappropriate.

The Shadow Side

This brings us to the shadow side of what it means to be a ONE. ONEs are deeply afraid of being bad, evil, angry, wrong, inappropriate, irresponsible, or condemned. This may have its roots in childhood: The ONE as a child felt a compulsion to be the "good" kid or felt extreme pressure to be "good." This shadow side can manifest itself in merit-based thinking, with a ONE believing that they "deserve" something or even that they "don't deserve" something. They may struggle with working alongside people who want something but haven't worked for it. This may lead them to withhold good things from people who don't "deserve" those things.

Some ONEs who haven't yet done their work may turn suppressed anger in on themselves and outward onto others in harmful ways. They may stew in anger, lack compassion and sympathy, and begin to voice the words of the Inner Critic in a detrimental way.

ONEs in Integration and Disintegration

The lines that connect the types on the Enneagram depict each type's movements in integration (growth, health, wellness) and disintegration (stress, unhealth, chaos). These movements can happen instantaneously as we become upset, or they can last for a season. Moving toward SEVEN (integration for a ONE) or FOUR (disintegration for a ONE) doesn't mean that the ONE becomes a SEVEN or FOUR, but rather that they take on the best or worst characteristics of the other type.

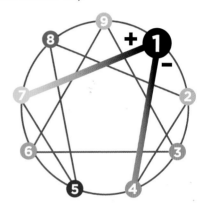

WARNING SIGNS

FEELING MISUNDERSTOOD

OVERLY SENSITIVE

EXTREME PRIDE

MOODY

PITY PARTY

CONTROLLING

RIGID MINDSET

STRESSED BY MESS

As ONEs begins to disintegrate, they move toward the unhealthy characteristics of type FOUR. They turn their anger inward, withdrawing, isolating, and engaging in deeply negative self-talk. They may become depressive, even clinically depressed, struggling with deep feelings of shame and guilt. Outwardly, they may speak to you in judgmental, correcting, condemning tones. They might throw themselves a pity party, marked by extreme pride and mood swings. They will likely become easily irritated or explosive and may erupt in anger quickly and uncharacteristically.

When ONEs do well, whether for a moment or a season, they move in integration toward type SEVEN. The ONEs who are able to silence their Inner Critic find joy, optimism, and freedom like the freewheeling, light-hearted SEVEN. They can tap into their childlike self, work hard without overthinking, set aside merit-based scorekeeping, and accept others for who they are. ONEs who are doing well can still work toward rightness and goodness with conviction, without the weight of condemnation. ONEs in integration look and feel lighter. They are unburdened by the weight of the world. They embody grace.

Digging Deeper into ONEs

ENNEADICTIONARY: HELPFUL ONE LANGUAGE

»——→ **Telos (n.):** Average ONEs are often drawn to a legalistic approach of black and white, right and wrong, good and bad. Healthy ONEs can focus on the *telos*, the purpose, intent, or goal, the ultimate result of an event or process. ONEs who have done their work can let go of imperfections in the present while they work toward the end goal. This *teleological* focus is a gift ONEs give to the world, because ONEs *do* actually know what is best and what needs to happen in order to improve, reform, and sometimes perfect the situation at hand.

SUBTYPES

»——→ **Social (SO) ONE:** SO ONEs are intellectual types who see their role as "teacher" to help others see what they already know—how to be perfect. They have high standards and a lot of self-control, and they live lives that set an example of integrity and principled conduct. They are systemic thinkers who focus on doing things well in a larger sense and model how to do things right for others. SO ONEs may seem FIVE-like in their actions, but internally they are focused on perfecting things rather than on energy conservation.

»——→ **Self-Preservation (SP) ONE:** SP ONEs are true perfectionists. They worry often, anticipate risks and problems, and focus on making everything they do more perfect. Their strong Inner Critic tells them they are highly flawed, and they are unsurprisingly very hard on themselves. They are more heady than other ONEs and more anxious and worried but also more friendly and warm. They are likely to be prepared and avoid expressing anger.

➠ **Sexual (SX) ONE:** SX ONEs are the countertype, meaning they present as a little less ONE-ish than the SP and SO ONEs. SX ONEs are zealous and idealistic. They are more reformers than perfectionists, and they tend to display more anger than other ONEs. They are idealistic about how things "should be," and they feel entitled to reform the world to their way. They focus less attention on reforming their own behavior and pay more attention to whether or not others are doing things "right." SX ONEs are very EIGHT-like.

WINGS

1W9   1W2

ONEs with a NINE wing (1w9) tend to be cooler, more relaxed, cerebral, impersonal, and objective. As a combination of two body types, they are more introverted and detached, likely because they are wrestling between what they ought to do and what will cause the fewest ripple effects in any given situation.

ONEs with a TWO wing (1w2) are an interesting combination of two types in the Dependent Stance. They tend to be more people-focused, warmer, and more helpful and sensitive. Yet they also may bend toward some of the vices of TWOs and will be more critical, fiery, vocal, controlling, and action-oriented than 1w9s.

TRIAD

All three types in the Body Triad (EIGHT, NINE, and ONE) take in information intuitively, through their bodies and wrestle with a desire for things to be set right. For ONEs, this means that they are driven by a strong internal sense of ethics. On the outside, ONEs may speak critically when things are not set right, while internally they are burning with a deep anger. This anger is not directed at a specific person, place, or thing but is a general anger that the world is not the way it ought to be.

Most ONEs are in denial of their own anger and would prefer to describe their feeling as resentment. ONEs who are asleep to their anger will often unexpectedly erupt on others or will fall victim to their anger as they burn in unfocused, unhelpful resentment. Yet one of the many gifts that healthy ONEs can give to the world is how they focus and use their anger. It truly is a gift to know what is right, what can be improved, and how to make the world better. ONEs who can learn to use their anger as fuel for their life and work will do great things because of the drive and motivation they have.

STANCE

ONEs, TWOs, and SIXes are in the Dependent Stance, meaning that they are oriented toward others and that their sense of identity comes from their relationships. ONEs are dependent externally to relationships with others and internally to their relationships with their thoughts.

All three Dependent Types believe that they must earn the right to have their needs met. They respond to problems, threats, and obstacles by conforming to an internalized set of rules, ideals, or codes of conduct. And since ONEs are both in the Dependent Stance *and* Body Triad, they will likely attempt to earn their right to autonomy and self-governance through being above reproach—by being "good."

ONEs are more oriented toward the present moment than other types. This gift also provides a growth path for ONEs. The more ONEs can become accepting of the unknown and not always having an answer, the more they will be opened up to growth. ONEs can relearn how to tolerate feelings of uncertainty without always referencing how things "should be." Make space for inevitable ambiguity.

MISSED CONNECTIONS

Here are the "missed connections" for ONE:

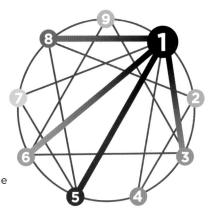

»→ **ONE and THREE:** ONEs and THREEs are united by their mutual drive for continuous improvement. They are literal, organized, and practical; have a strong work ethic; and have a "holy discontent" (are rightly dissatisfied) with things that are merely adequate. Both struggle with repressing emotions while at the same time feeling very deeply.

»→ **ONE and FIVE:** ONEs and FIVEs are hardworking types with strong work ethics. They are dependable and reliable people. Neither will cut corners for the sake of time. Rules matter for them, and boundaries are encouraged.

»→ **ONE and SIX:** ONEs and SIXes value "rightness" and see a proper way of doing things. Rules and hierarchy matter. Both types struggle with paranoia and self-doubt. Both are committed, reliable, and responsible.

»→ **ONE and EIGHT:** ONEs and EIGHTs have a very strong sense of justice and ethics and will work hard to achieve it. Both types will get very fiery when something isn't "right." Both are argumentative and can be perceived as very intense people. They feel things physically, hate being manipulated, and experience anger very deeply.

If You Love a ONE

Chance are that by now you have identified some ONEs in your life, or maybe you're reading this because you know a loved one is a ONE. So, if you love a ONE, here are a few things to keep in mind:

»→ **They need help stopping.** ONEs are constantly on the move. When they aren't physically working toward the next project, they are mentally processing the latest book they read. They wake in the morning with a headache because their brain was working on overdrive during the night. They frown while you're talking because their Inner Critic is yelling at them. Help them stop. Give them safe space to unwind, both in your posture with them and in your physical environment. Move them toward nature (see page 37), where they will find grace in the natural world. Take something off their plate so that they can feel permitted to stop. But please note that you may need to first listen to their worries and concerns before they can stop.

»→ **Be specific.** Since ONEs are very in touch with their sense of right and wrong, they give feedback very specifically and prefer receiving specific feedback. Since their tendency is to see everything that is wrong with something they do, ONEs tend not to value blanket statements like "Great job!" or "I'm sorry!" and will only believe your feedback if it's precise.

»→ **Help them with expectation management.** ONEs need to be reminded in practical, specific, tangible, logical ways that you are not expecting them to be perfect. They have incredibly high standards for themselves. While you can't change their own standards, make sure they know that you don't hold them to perfection. They need to know that it is okay to make mistakes and that you will still love them unconditionally. Tell them you love them for who they are and not for how "good" they are. Then show them. Then tell them again.

»→ **Be fair.** ONEs work hard until the job is done. If you live with a ONE, make sure you do your fair share of the responsibilities so that the ONE isn't left with all of the work.

1

The Way Forward

None of us exist in the world in a vacuum. As a ONE, one of the core lies that you need to name and unlearn is that you are more broken than everyone else and that you can fix your brokenness with hard work. When these lies start to pop up, practice replacing them with these truths:

»—→ **LIE: It's not okay to make a mistake.** TRUTH: Not everything is on your shoulders. Mistakes can usually be undone or apologized for. Making a mistake doesn't negate your good work.

»—→ **LIE: Everything has to be done my way.** TRUTH: You do often know a really good way of doing things, but there is more than one way to get the job done. Part of being a human means that we live in a community, and part of how you can love others is by conceding and compromising your way for theirs.

»—→ **LIE: In every area in which I'm failing, others have to pay the price.** TRUTH: Your failure usually doesn't impact others as much as you think it does. You *are* important but not always as important as you think you are.

»—→ **LIE: Perfection is possible.** TRUTH: You can swap your pursuit of perfection with your pursuit of *telos*. You can be "in process" and still be doing good work.

»—→ **LIE: I am not good.** TRUTH: You are worthy and loved no matter what you do.

RIPPLE EFFECTS

The way you show up in the world has real impact and ripple effects on other people.

»—→ Every time you project your high set of expectations onto other people without caution, care, and concern, you risk damaging your relationships with them. Perfection is not the goal and is not attainable anyway, because all humans are flawed. Every time you find fault in others, you weaken your relationship with them. Learn to love the people around you for exactly who they are, rather than who you want them to be.

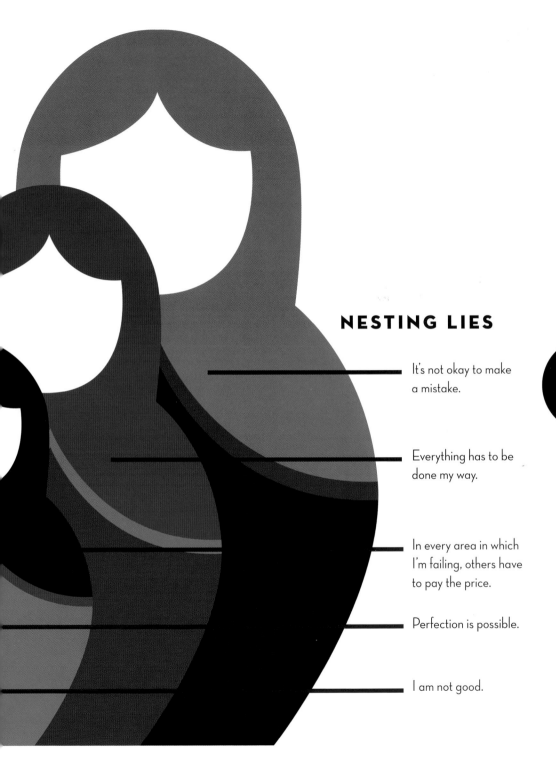

NESTING LIES

It's not okay to make a mistake.

Everything has to be done my way.

In every area in which I'm failing, others have to pay the price.

Perfection is possible.

I am not good.

1

»—→ Every time you overextend yourself by taking responsibility of things that are not yours to be responsible for, you start down a path toward resenting things, people, and yourself. Cultivate healthy boundaries of your responsibilities. Trust others to do their work, and don't do it for them.

»—→ You do not need to be right all the time. Every time you focus more on being right than on the people around you, you minimize their humanity and glorify your own. Give people space to think and work things out for themselves. Even if you are right, take the role of teacher and help people come to their own conclusions. Give and receive grace in your relationships.

SELF CARE FOR ONES

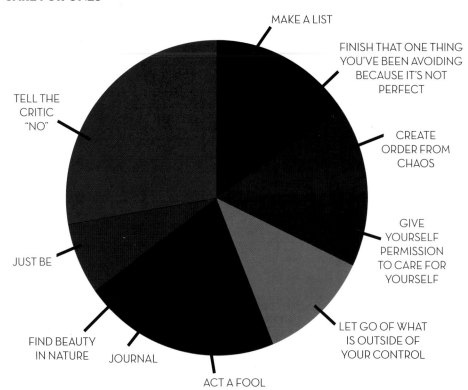

MAKE A LIST

FINISH THAT ONE THING YOU'VE BEEN AVOIDING BECAUSE IT'S NOT PERFECT

CREATE ORDER FROM CHAOS

GIVE YOURSELF PERMISSION TO CARE FOR YOURSELF

LET GO OF WHAT IS OUTSIDE OF YOUR CONTROL

ACT A FOOL

JOURNAL

FIND BEAUTY IN NATURE

JUST BE

TELL THE CRITIC "NO"

- **Tell the critic no.** You are not powerless against your Inner Critic. Our ONE friends suggest practices such as writing down what your Inner Critic says to learn its voice and begin to distinguish it from your own thoughts. You may need to change your posture or say "no" out loud.

- **Nature.** In nature, ONEs can let go of what is "right" and what is "wrong" because nature invites you to dismantle your view of right and wrong and trade it in for a new hierarchy based on beauty and wonder. Slow down in nature and reconnect with yourself and the created world.

> This *teleological* focus is a gift ONEs give to the world, because ONEs *do* actually know what is best and what needs to happen in order to improve, reform, and sometimes perfect the situation at hand.

- **Journaling.** Write down the cries of your heart and get them out of your head. Confront your Inner Critic on paper. Read your words back to yourself and learn from yourself.

- **Challenge your definition of right and wrong.** Challenge yourself by asking some deeper, more probing questions. Ask what happens if you right all of the wrongs you see. Ask if there is more than one truth present at the same time. Ask if someone else's version of the truth has equal merit to yours, and be willing to compromise.

- **Adopt the Three Ss—Silence, Solitude, and Stillness.** ONEs will find this three-part practice to be more challenging than other types, but they also need the Three Ss more than other types. Meditating on words, sacred texts, songs, or other concepts that are proven faithful and true will give your mind something to do while you are practicing the Three Ss. Learn to just be, to let go, to be fully present in solitude, silence, and stillness.

- **Act a fool.** No matter your age, profession, role, or responsibilities, we give you permission (and in fact encourage you!) to act a fool. Sing karaoke, joke around with friends, somersault down a hill, join that ultimate frisbee league, stop working, have fun, and act a fool. Jolt yourself into your SEVEN space of integration with something silly.

BODY

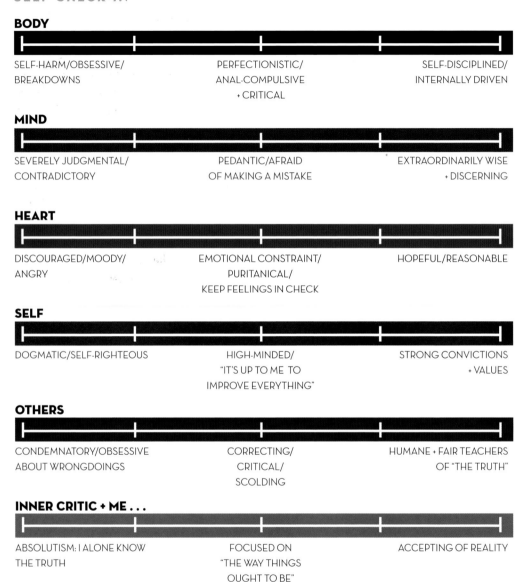

SELF-HARM/OBSESSIVE/
BREAKDOWNS

PERFECTIONISTIC/
ANAL-COMPULSIVE
+ CRITICAL

SELF-DISCIPLINED/
INTERNALLY DRIVEN

MIND

SEVERELY JUDGMENTAL/
CONTRADICTORY

PEDANTIC/AFRAID
OF MAKING A MISTAKE

EXTRAORDINARILY WISE
+ DISCERNING

HEART

DISCOURAGED/MOODY/
ANGRY

EMOTIONAL CONSTRAINT/
PURITANICAL/
KEEP FEELINGS IN CHECK

HOPEFUL/REASONABLE

SELF

DOGMATIC/SELF-RIGHTEOUS

HIGH-MINDED/
"IT'S UP TO ME TO
IMPROVE EVERYTHING"

STRONG CONVICTIONS
+ VALUES

OTHERS

CONDEMNATORY/OBSESSIVE
ABOUT WRONGDOINGS

CORRECTING/
CRITICAL/
SCOLDING

HUMANE + FAIR TEACHERS
OF "THE TRUTH"

INNER CRITIC + ME . . .

ABSOLUTISM: I ALONE KNOW
THE TRUTH

FOCUSED ON
"THE WAY THINGS
OUGHT TO BE"

ACCEPTING OF REALITY

The Reckoning

It is imperative that, at some point along the journey, ONEs realize their standards of perfection are unrealistic and unattainable, yet they are still loved. As with any other type, a ONE's reckoning can come either the easy way or the hard way. It may come in the way of your resentment with yourself, others, and the world building up so much that it reaches a breaking point. It may come by years of being rigid and inflexible in your ideals. It may come in the form of slowly and unintentionally pushing everybody away because they don't live up to your standards. Alternatively, you can make the hard choice of embracing the mess both inside yourself and around you, being satisfied with progress over perfection, and learning to recognize the Inner Critic for what it is.

This shift will be difficult and paradigmatic, which is why it is your reckoning. ONEs need to hear, see, feel, and believe that they are loved for who they are and not for how "good" they are. It is okay to make mistakes—all humans do. No one is expecting you to be as perfect as you expect yourself to be. The good news for ONEs is that there is so much more grace for you than you realize, and it's freeing for you and the people in your life. The more you learn to extend yourself grace in small ways, the more you will learn to be free from the tendencies that hold you back from true growth and connection with others.

1

TYPE

TWO

The Helper / Giver / Befriender

An Enneagram TWO is called the Helper, the Giver, or the Befriender. They are thoughtful, pleasant, approachable, friendly, resourceful, and service-oriented people. TWOs have a very keen ability to anticipate the needs of anybody around them, and they have a greater capacity than most people to personally meet those needs themselves. They love being a part of the lives of others, make great friends, are great listeners, and, in general, are very aware of the people in their lives. TWOs make great companions, assistants, and seconds-in-command, as they are bent toward helping others accomplish whatever they need.

TWOs can come across as generous and selfless people, but there are a lot of hidden expectations and ulterior motives underneath the surface that others can't see—TWOs themselves often lack self-awareness underneath the surface.

A World of TWOs

The world would be a more peaceful, kind, and empathetic place full of complex contradictions. There would be less loneliness in the world, as everyone would be seen and loved. There would be no unmet needs. On the other hand, there would be chaos, as no one would have boundaries. People would concern themselves with how other people were doing, and everyone would compete to out-love one another, never taking care of themselves. In general, nothing would be accomplished because everyone would be paralyzed between the desire to help and the desire to see the leadership needs met. The world would be full of exhausted listeners who are never fully heard and people who are taken care of and yet feel completely neglected all at the same time.

Motivation

TWOs have a compulsion to be helpful or necessary in any given situation, especially to the people they love. If you're ever in a situation where you need someone to run an errand, or be a listening ear, TWOs will see it as their personal duty to be the one who comes in to save the day.

While this compulsion exists in small ways that vary for each TWO, it's even more pronounced in the big needs of life. TWOs work hard to be that trusted friend who will drop everything at a moment's notice for you, that reliable employee who you can bounce ideas off of and will deliver in clutch situations, that close companion who knows and anticipates your needs before you can say them out loud. Many TWOs are masters at making themselves essential pieces of every equation that's important to them.

The Shadow Side

As with any other type, the compulsion of a TWO comes from a deeper place of need. Rather than believing that they are already loved and celebrated for who they are, TWOs settle for being needed. Being necessary in any situation is the path that TWOs choose toward earning love and believing in their own worth. Some suggest that this motivation comes from early childhood wounds of feeling neglected or forced into caretaking positions. Others suggest that it's a posture toward the rest of the world that TWOs are born with. Either way, this disposition is one that is so ingrained in TWOs that they're completely unaware of the internal motivations behind their actions.

Pride is at the root of the TWO's shadow side. Many people are surprised when they first learn that pride dictates so much of a TWO's behavior when, on the surface, TWOs are always focused on others, neglecting their own needs and desires and giving freely and generously. However, once you dig a bit beneath the surface, you'll see that a TWO's giving is anything but free. There is almost always a string attached to the others-focused acts of TWOs, even if it's as simple as recognition, making their image more favorable, or gratitude. TWOs are frequently unaware of these expectations that they have of others, but the point remains that they can compulsively help, give, and serve with hopes of personal gain. They want to be seen and appreciated, they want to receive as lavishly as they are capable of giving, they expect people to simply *know* their desires and needs without expressing them, and they want to be known as *the* trustworthy, faithful, self-sacrificing person above everyone else.

If you have a hard time believing that TWOs are motivated by pride, watch them when they're used to a certain person coming to them for advice, assistance, or a tangible favor whenever they need it, only to see that person go to somebody else for that same sort of help. TWOs, on autopilot, can care more about being *the* person to meet the needs of their loved ones than they do about the needs of the loved ones actually being met.

2

TWOs in Integration and Disintegration

When TWOs are in stress, whether it be a single moment or in a general season of life, they move toward the characteristics of EIGHTs. They become less accommodating and more direct and controlling, less polite and more aggressive, and less patient and quicker to cut people off. Their general disposition to come alongside others in assistance becomes an orientation against other people. When they're not doing well, they can easily bulldoze over anybody who gets in their way and feel vindicated in doing so. They are more likely to take charge than to take a back seat. It is worth noting that moving toward EIGHT in stress is not always a negative experience, because not all stress leads to disaster. For instance, if a TWO is under a time crunch for a project or event, they are able drop the need to be accommodating and instead be commanding and assertive in such a way that people will follow. TWOs, like any other type, have a choice any time they are in a stressful situation or season whether they'll respond in a way that is helpful or in a way that is self-serving.

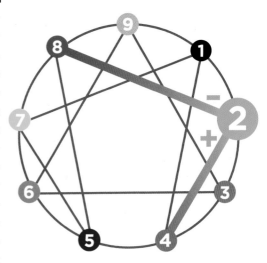

WARNING SIGNS

PASSIVE-AGGRESSIVE

NEGATIVE SELF-TALK

PICKING FIGHTS

BITTERNESS

DEMANDING

COMBATIVE

NEEDY/HOVERING

MANIPULATIVE/ CONTROLLING

TWOs in health move toward the characteristics of FOURs. It is a sign of growth when a TWO can take all of the energy that they always focus outward and turn it inward to actually pay attention to themselves. Integration for TWOs looks like identifying their feelings, needs, and desires and being able to express them exactly as they are, even if they can be perceived as negative or uncomfortable. They are unafraid of showing their rough edges. Healthy TWOs embrace vulnerability and risk coming across as "needy." They are able to sit with themselves and their feelings and actually understand why they do everything that they do. When TWOs live in this awareness, they can give, love, and serve out of an assurance in who they are, rather than as a means of validation. It is then that TWOs can truly give freely and generously, loving others just as they are. For many TWOs, learning that their path to growth involves paying attention to their own desires and needs can seem jarring. It is easy for TWOs to hear all of this as selfish. However, it is *crucial* for TWOs to know this: YOU influence every single relationship you have, so learning about yourself and caring for yourself is actually in the best interest of everybody you know and love.

Digging Deeper into TWOs
ENNEADICTIONARY: HELPFUL TWO LANGUAGE

»⟶ **Social Temperature (n.):** TWOs are continually gauging the social temperature and wind direction because they base their identity on how others are disposed toward them and react to them.

»⟶ **Martyr (n.):** TWOs understand and anticipate other people's needs, feelings, and desires more than almost anybody else does, so they can care very well for the people in their lives. However, TWOs can expect others to treat them the same way without communicating those expectations, so they often see themselves as martyrs, describing how they will go to whatever length needed for people who "don't even notice or care."

»⟶ **Savior Complex (n.):** Nobody will get excited at an SOS message like a TWO will. TWOs thrive off of being the necessary part of someone's life and can easily fall into the trap that people *need* them to survive. TWOs will go to extreme lengths to be the savior that they think other people need, and they hope to be recognized as such.

SUBTYPES
»⟶ **Self-Preservation (SP) TWO:** SP TWOs are more inclined to work behind the scenes than the other TWO subtypes. They pay attention to the small and practical details and channel their service to others through that lens. SP TWOs will make sure that you're well rested, well fed, and well cared for in the details that you may not be

2

paying attention to yourself. Physical proximity to the people they love is a high value for them. SP TWOs are the countertype, so they are often less socially assertive, less expressive, and more likely to withdraw than other TWOs. Due to the SP Instinct being focused on preserving energy and tangible resources, SP TWOs can also be more self-indulgent than other TWOs.

»—→ **Sexual (SX) TWO:** All SX types find their security through building strong, intimate relationships. SX TWOs do this by going out of their way to be winsome, generous, and attentive to people they find desirable. They will perform grand gestures, dive deeply and quickly into getting to know someone and their needs, and in general give lots of social attention to win people over. SX TWOs are passionate, persistent, and highly adaptable. While all TWOs struggle with the idea of boundaries, SX TWOs in particular have a hard time accepting no for an answer and find it difficult to believe that their way of showing care can be overwhelming to others.

»—→ **Social (SO) TWO:** SO TWOs gravitate more naturally toward positions of leadership or influence than the other TWO subtypes. They are masters of spinning intricate social webs around themselves where they aren't necessarily the star of the show at all times, but they always know how to be close to the action and have a hand in everything that's important to them. Having a wide variety of connections is of very high value for SO TWOs. They like to have people in their corner everywhere they go, and they use their awareness of others' needs and desires as a means of deepening these connections. Making this wide network of people can often be a method of overcompensating for the fear that they are not actually lovable enough on their own.

WINGS

2W1   2W3

What's Your Enneatype?

TWOs with a ONE wing (2w1) are a combination of two dependent types, so they are less likely to make a splash than 2w3s. They are dutiful, rule-oriented, and objective, more likely to direct their service behind the scenes than 2w3s. The TWO tendency to see themselves as martyrs combined with the high moral standard of ONEs can make 2w1s more resentful or judgmental.

TWOs with a THREE wing (2w3) are a combination of two Heart Triad types and as such are much more image conscious and aware of the social rules. They are socially assertive, competent, charming, and seemingly self-assured. They are more competitive than 2w1s and will also have a harder time being receptive to criticism.

TRIAD

TWOs, along with THREEs and FOURs, are part of the Heart Triad, which means that they take in information from their emotional centers. Regardless of whether they're aware of it or not, TWOs at first respond emotionally to everything that they encounter. This tendency does not mean that TWOs are incapable of critical thought or decisive action, but those methods are not the first responses for TWOs. The Heart Triad is the most image conscious of all three triads. For TWOs, this looks like the constant awareness of how they can fill the needs in the room, putting a lot of emotional stock in whether or not people like them, and frustration when they don't get the recognition that they look for. Shame is also a motivator for the three types in the Heart Triad, and TWOs overcompensate for their fear of feeling worthless by doing everything they can to make themselves useful. These types also all experience themselves in relation to other people, for better or for worse.

STANCE

TWOs, along with ONEs and SIXes, are in the Dependent Stance. All three types are oriented toward other people, as well as being dependent on others. They all find their sense of identity outside of themselves. The types in the Dependent Stance feel and act more instinctually than they think in productive ways; hence they are known as "thinking-repressed." Because they're oriented toward others, they can have a hard time thinking for themselves without the opinions of everyone around them. For TWOs, being in the Dependent Stance looks like drawing your whole identity from the roles you play in the lives of others. They can struggle to find a strong sense of self because they are always filling relational holes around them rather than trying to find their own autonomy.

Here are the "missed connections" for TWO:

»—→ **TWO and FIVE:** These types do not have that much in common at all. TWOs are compulsive givers, while FIVEs are compulsive takers. However, both types struggle with asking for help when they are truly in a vulnerable place. Neither type wants to have to depend on others.

»—→ **TWO and SIX:** TWOs and SIXes both show up in the world in similar ways. They love people deeply and will do anything for their people. They are safe people to talk to and are always present. They love to have people around them, and both love building strong relationships. Both types care for and champion other people.

»—→ **TWO and SEVEN:** Both types are very open to the world. They both have a childlike way of showing up in the environments around them. SEVENs have a childlike joy and lightness, and TWOs can tend toward a childlike dependence in relationships. Both types struggle with the fear of missing out and are adept at curating social experiences.

»—→ **TWO and NINE:** These are both self-forgetting types. While NINEs merge to keep the peace (and to be left alone), thus forgetting themselves, TWOs hide behind others with more dominant personalities to find value in themselves and their relationships. Both types are empathetic, generous, serving types of people, and they may struggle with saying no.

If You Love a TWO

Odds are that there is at least one significant TWO in your life whom you have loved for some time, but if you're new to the Enneagram, everything under the surface may come as a big surprise to you. A wonderful part of the Enneagram is that it gives us the knowledge that shows us how to love people better. Here are five things to bear in mind about how to best care for the TWOs in your life.

»⟶ **Make it clear that they are a priority.** TWOs are very good at prioritizing other people and making them feel loved, cared for, and important. They often have the underlying thought that nobody cares about them the way that they care about other people. TWOs often don't know how to receive generosity that they feel like they haven't earned, but it's important to show them this generosity nonetheless. Ask them to hang out, do something just because they like it, go out of your way to see them, talk to them about things that you know they care about, or throw them a party on their birthday. It is a good reminder for TWOs that other people are capable of loving this way and that it's okay for them to receive it.

»⟶ **Be specific when you thank or praise them.** Many TWOs struggle with feeling taken for granted, and they fear that people don't actually notice or appreciate all that they do. Simply saying "Thank you!" or "Good job!" is nice, but it does not show a TWO that you see them or appreciate them. TWOs want to feel seen, and you can do this by being clear in your positive feedback to them.

»⟶ **"It's not about you."** Remember that the core vice of TWOs is pride, and they can seemingly take it personally if a friend goes to someone else for help or advice, deals with a problem or difficult situation on their own, or somehow doesn't involve the TWO in the process. TWOs need to be lovingly reminded that not every decision or situation in the lives of the people they love needs to be run past them first. This is a challenging message for TWOs to hear. Lovingly coming alongside them and reminding them of this truth is a great way to help TWOs to combat this unhealthy compulsion of theirs.

»⟶ **Help them remember their limits.** TWOs like to live as if they don't have limits. They like to think that they can help with every task, say yes to everything that comes their way, make space for everyone in their life, and do everything that needs to be done. It is really challenging for TWOs to embrace their own capacity. TWOs need help to understand their own limits. They need you to provide tangible assistance when they don't ask for it. They may need you to take things entirely off their plate. They may need very loud and persistent reminders to slow down. It really is beneficial for them and for you when they can have a healthy understanding of their own capacity, and they most likely need help to see it.

TWOs need you to prioritize them and be generous with them but also to challenge them and pay attention to the things that they won't pay attention to themselves.

The Way Forward

If we go way back to the lies that we believe about ourselves, we'll see that each one can be countered with the truth that will help us be released from the boxes that we build around ourselves for our whole lives. We need these truths spoken to us again and again.

»→ **LIE: It's not okay to be needy or to have needs.** TRUTH: You do, in fact, have needs, and it is more than okay. It makes you human, just like everyone else. With needs come the opportunity to receive love and generosity from others, which is a wonderful thing.

»→ **LIE: I am only valuable if people need me.** TRUTH: You are valuable no matter what. Nothing can change that.

»→ **LIE: I can only be happy if I make others happy.** TRUTH: It is more than okay for other people to be the ones making you happy.

»→ **LIE: With enough love, I can save anyone.** TRUTH: You were not meant to be the person to save anyone, and you're not capable of saving them, which is okay. You can love them fiercely anyway.

»→ **LIE: I am not loved for who I am.** TRUTH: You are loved just for being you, no strings attached.

RIPPLE EFFECTS

Your actions and tendencies have an influence on more people than just you, and it's better for everyone when you pay attention to this influence.

»→ When you offer help that isn't yours to give or insert yourself into a situation where you're not needed, know that it can make the other person or people feel smothered, overwhelmed, disrespected, frustrated, and/or unheard. Even if your intentions aren't self-seeking, the impact of your actions communicate that you don't trust the person's decision-making and that you believe yourself to be the necessary solution. This situation is actually not helpful for you or them.

»→ Remember that you are not limitless. When you think that you can give, give, give without acknowledging your own needs or capacity, you are diminishing the quality of what you're giving to

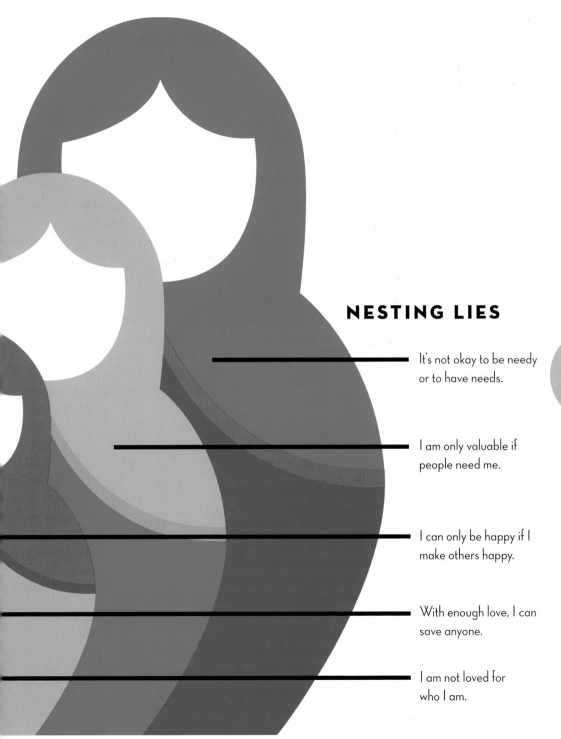

NESTING LIES

It's not okay to be needy or to have needs.

I am only valuable if people need me.

I can only be happy if I make others happy.

With enough love, I can save anyone.

I am not loved for who I am.

2

everybody, and oftentimes they can tell. The people in your life deserve better than to receive you running on fumes. Everyone loses when you don't embrace your own limits.

»——→ When you don't pay attention to your own desires or feelings, they eventually will bottle up and come out in the martyr-like rage you've read about, and this is not fair to the people you care about. As a TWO, you can have very high expectations of the people in your life that are often subconscious, but when they are subconscious, that means that these expectations won't be communicated. From someone else's point of view, you are giving, caring, and serving like always until you snap and reveal the previously invisible unmet expectations. There are consequences to ignoring your own emotional needs and desires.

HEALTHY PRACTICES

»——→ **Hospitality.** Regardless of whether or not you have people over at your own home, you have the opportunity to be hospitable to people anywhere you go. TWOs are naturally bent toward serving and paying attention to the needs of others, so it is a good, natural practice for TWOs to continue to make space for others in their homes, neighborhoods, workplaces, and communities. The important practice here is to assume the humble posture of hospitality, truly seeking the best for others without any expectations.

»——→ **Solitude.** TWOs are very others-oriented in all that they do, and they have a hard time knowing who they are or what their purpose is outside the context of other people. Solitude invites you to simply *be* without needing to do anything for anybody.

»——→ **Journaling.** TWOs are naturally disconnected from their own deep thoughts and feelings, and it takes a lot of conscious effort for them to get in touch with those parts of themselves. Journaling helps TWOs externalize their thoughts, fears, joys, frustrations, hopes, and desires. Journaling provides the space to name, claim, and sit with everything that's going on inside of you, rather than looking for validation from others to fill this void.

SELF-CARE FOR TWOS

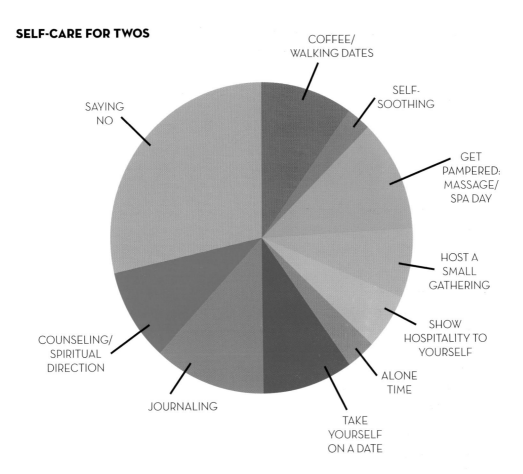

COFFEE/
WALKING DATES

SELF-
SOOTHING

GET
PAMPERED:
MASSAGE/
SPA DAY

HOST A
SMALL
GATHERING

SHOW
HOSPITALITY TO
YOURSELF

ALONE
TIME

TAKE
YOURSELF
ON A DATE

JOURNALING

COUNSELING/
SPIRITUAL
DIRECTION

SAYING
NO

2

BODY

ABUSE FOOD/SOMATIZATION OF
AGGRESSIONS

WEAR OUT SELF FOR OTHERS

SERVICE-ORIENTED/
FOCUSED ON SELF-CARE

MIND

RATIONALIZING/SENDING
DOUBLE MESSAGES

OVER-THINKING/
FULL OF "GOOD INTENTIONS"

THOUGHTFUL/THINKING OF
OTHERS

HEART

RESENTFUL/ANGRY

OVERLY INTIMATE/
FIXATED ON LOVE

HUMBLE/ALTRUISTIC/
COMPASSIONATE

SELF

SELF-DECEPTIVE ABOUT MOTIVES
AND BEHAVIOR

SELF-IMPORTANT/
INFLATED VIEW OF SELF

LOVING TOWARDS SELF

OTHERS

MANIPULATIVE/UNDERMINING/
ENTITLED

BECOME A "MARTYR"/
PATRONIZING/PRESUMPTUOUS

NSELFISH/ALTRUISTIC/
UNCONDITIONAL

WHEN ASKED "HOW ARE YOU?"

PANIC + DEFLECT

SHALLOW RESPONSE +
MAYBE DEFLECT

PAUSE, REFLECT +
RESPOND HONESTLY

The Reckoning

The reckoning for each TWO looks different, but the point of it is that you are no longer able to endlessly serve, give, care, or be available like you are accustomed to. This reckoning could look like isolation, when you are removed from all sorts of people and have nobody to draw purpose or identity from. It could look like being in a position where you have to be completely at the mercy of the generosity of others, not being able to pull strings or earn your way to anything. Perhaps it would be some other way of having to come to grips with who you are as a person without being able to rely on any of the methods you've used in the past to define yourself. Should you be in a position to receive it, these reckonings will make you a healthier, more self-aware, and more integrated person than you were before.

Now, as with every other type, the reckoning is not always necessary for you to learn your lesson. We are all faced with the choice of learning our path forward the simple way or the long, challenging way. Fortunately, you have the opportunity to take the smoother path every single day. That's not to say that it won't be hard, because it takes work to slow down and stop giving endlessly. It takes effort to pay attention to the deeper parts of yourself. It takes strength and humility to confront your own prideful or manipulative intentions. Going against the grain of your autopilot self is always going to be challenging, but this path is where you find your freedom.

2

TYPE
THREE

The Achiever / Performer / Motivator

Enneagram THREEs

are the achievers. They are hardworking, assertive, task-oriented, ambitious, charming, resourceful, adaptable, and capable people. THREEs have a natural ability to walk into a room, identify whom they need to impress, and know exactly how to do so. They can play all sorts of roles in work, relationships, and organizational settings because of this superpower. In general, THREEs have a higher capacity to achieve and accomplish than most people do. They make great coaches and motivators because in addition to knowing their own path to success, they also know how *others* can succeed in achieving their goals. THREEs thrive in situations with lists and measurable outcomes.

While most THREEs can come across as strong, competent, and confident people, they often are merely projecting that image as a defense mechanism to avoid doubts and fears about their own worth, strength, and ability. They can effortlessly rotate between all of the different masks that they wear, each one catering to whatever the situation requires. This ability can certainly be helpful at times, but THREEs often use it because they are hesitant to show the world the real person behind the mask or because they don't even know who they are once you remove all of the masks.

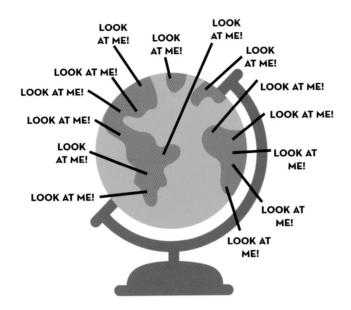

A World of THREEs

The world would be organized, efficient, and productive. People would be decisive and direct, and emotions would not get in the way of decision-making. Stuff would get done, plain and simple. However, with so many people succeeding, success would become meaningless. Chaos would ensue as everyone would strive way too hard to be seen, and there would be nobody there to ascribe value to hard work. People would choose productivity over emotional health, over each other, and over the greater good. The world would become weary with the facades, and vulnerability would become a hot commodity.

Motivation

THREEs have a compulsion to be successful and productive. Any situation can be turned into a task that a THREE knows how to win. They know all of the unwritten, unspoken rules of how to succeed in school, at work, and in their communities. They pick up on the slightest details of social encounters and subconsciously register what others do that work and don't work. A THREE will notice the person who is the most influential and the positive- and negative-response things they do. They will notice which group seems to have more energy and what fuels their energy. THREEs have an unnaturally good read on such social dynamics and, as a result, can find themselves with an entire menu of options for how they want to show up in a given space or conversation. This ability also helps many THREEs be highly productive and achieve results in whatever it is that they're trying to accomplish. If they are not able to achieve said results, they are then at least able to convey the image that they are producing results.

The Shadow Side

In their pursuit of finding love and belonging, THREEs settle for being admired. They mistake being impressive, strong, talented, and successful for being worthy of love. Gaining the respect and admiration of others is a survival strategy for THREEs that when unchecked can also become their sole purpose. Without even realizing it, THREEs can spend much of their energy on being funny, smart, talented, resourceful, attractive, or whatever else the situation calls for— to the point that a THREE won't even know who they really are because they have wrapped so much of their identity in other people's desires and expectations.

THREEs fall for several traps that lead to these unhealthy and tiring cycles and compulsions. These traps include but are not limited to the ideas that it's not okay to be flawed; that they must be "on" at all times; that people only love them for what they *do* rather than for who they *are*; that their sole purpose in life is doing, accomplishing, and climbing up social ladders; that there is nobody there underneath all of the masks that they wear; and that they are inherently unworthy. Somewhere early on in the life of a THREE, they found that people will give them praise if they do what they are "supposed" to do. This behavior is often given positive reinforcement and/or serves as a way to cope with some harder situations in life. With so many merit-based societal systems in place, it can be very easy for THREEs to believe that the only value they have is in what they do, accomplish, or contribute. A whole life of this behavior can leave a THREE completely chained to the pursuit of success, admiration, accomplishment, and fulfilling spoken and unspoken expectations.

Tied up in all of these traps is the core vice for THREEs: deceit. This vice does not necessarily imply that all THREEs are pathological liars, but a core part of their survival strategy involves altering some or all of what they say or how they come across, even if it's not actually true to who they are. This tendency can spiral completely out of control and result in THREEs living wildly different lives that change based on who they're around, always being afraid to tell the truth, or becoming addicted to materialism. However, this vice often shows up in much smaller, more subtle ways. THREEs can naturally (sometimes subconsciously) reframe reality to present themselves in a much more favorable light, erasing their rough edges and editing uglier parts of their narrative to hide the truth. They often don't do this reframing with malicious intent, as they can subconsciously deceive themselves from believing more uncomfortable aspects of their lives. THREEs can change their internal and external narratives very frequently based on whatever serves them best in the moment. Much of this deceit stems from the fear of being rejected if they were to show any sort of flaw or blemish at all.

THREEs in Integration and Disintegration

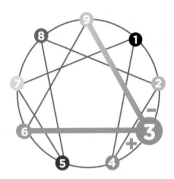

When THREEs move into stress or disintegration, they take on some of the characteristics of NINEs. Their normal ability to be decisive and take action is dulled, and they fall into patterns of lethargy and sloth. This movement can be triggered in a single moment, or it can be a response to a general season of stress and unrest in their life. They can become withdrawn, act on autopilot, become disengaged, lose their usual drive, and become very hesitant to disclose anything that could potentially rock the boat. When THREEs aren't doing well, they see a long list of obstacles and challenges and become overwhelmed by them rather than motivated by them. THREEs can respond to stressful situations in ways that are helpful to others by using some of their NINE tendencies.

Healthy THREEs move toward the positive side of SIXes. They take their ability to achieve and win people over and use it for the improvement of their groups or communities as a whole. They can be generous, cooperative, committed to the feelings and well-being of others, vulnerable, and committed to finding and telling the truth, rather than altering narratives based on what's convenient. They courageously acknowledge their fears of rejection and worthlessness and pursue authenticity. THREEs in health recognize that their success and well-being is contingent on the success and well-being of the people around them, so they use their superpowers of winsomeness, achievement, and efficiency for the sake of causes bigger than their own personal agendas or five-year plans. They have the ability to become the glue that keeps groups and communities together.

WARNING SIGNS

LIVING LIFE ON AUTOPILOT

IMPATIENT

AVOIDING EMOTIONS

ANGRY/SHORT

INTENSE ANXIETY

NUMBING BEHAVIORS

WITHDRAWING

PRETENDING TO BE BUSY

Digging Deeper into THREEs

»→ **Branding (v.):** THREEs are the most image-conscious type and are always aware of the image or "brand" they are putting on display to the world around them. THREEs are among the most diverse of the types because their brand can take many forms. Their brand is often determined by what is viewed as successful or good in a given environment, and they are sure to act in line with their brand, whatever it is.

»→ **Impostor Syndrome (n.):** A persistent internalized fear of being exposed as a fraud. In their journey inward, THREEs have to overcome their deep but ungrounded anxiety that behind their roles and masks, there may not be any true self at all.

»→ **Power Radar (n.):** THREEs have a superpower of being able to walk into a room and identify the person or group of people who carries the most influence. They are then able to identify whatever is necessary to win those people over. This impulse can help THREEs out in many situations, but when unchecked, they can become slaves to it.

SUBTYPES

»→ **Self-Preservation (SP) THREE:** SP THREEs are more likely to avoid the spotlight than the other two THREE subtypes, preferring to do work behind the scenes. They are organized, efficient, and highly practical. They have a high value for getting things done and want to be recognized for all of their hard work and contributions. SP THREEs may act as if they don't want the praise and admiration for being the star of the show, but they absolutely want to get credit for the work that they put in, often making a point to subtly bring up whatever they have contributed. SP THREEs are the countertype; they are not as obvious in asserting their presence as the other two subtypes, often choosing a more reserved, calculated approach to gaining the approval of others. Due to their reliance on tasks and productivity to gain the approval of others, SP THREEs can easily fall into workaholism if they aren't careful.

»→ **Sexual (SX) THREE:** SX THREEs are prone to taking their winsome tendencies and zooming in on one person at a time to become whatever that person finds to be appealing. SX THREEs, like most of the other SX types, are intense and competitive, very capable of filling a whole room with their personalities. Relationships are often the vehicle for SX THREEs to find their own validation and success. More than other THREEs, SX THREEs want to be associated with others who are successful or influential in one way or another because they see the success and admiration of the people close to them as a reflection of their own success and admiration. They can also use this orientation toward relationships as a way to be supportive and loyal to their people.

⟫→ **Social (SO) THREE:** SO THREEs are more inclined to be the center of attention than the other two THREE subtypes. Gathering people around them who will help them achieve their goals and look successful comes very naturally to SO THREEs. They are also very capable of captivating a whole room and inspiring people toward a common goal or purpose. But SO THREEs always have their radar on to sense if any negative feedback may be coming their way. They want everyone to know about their skills and accomplishments and are very drawn to places of influence, for better or for worse.

WINGS

3W2   3W4

THREEs with a TWO wing (3w2) are more oriented toward relationships than 3w4s. They are warm, encouraging, and likeable. They enjoy being the center of attention and can be manipulative. 3w2s are more invested in the lives of the people close to them and can fall into seeing themselves as their loved ones' heroes. They are much more disconnected from their feelings than 3w4s.

THREEs with a FOUR wing (3w4) are less focused on people and more focused on work, success, and introspection. They are usually more sensitive, artistic, imaginative, articulate, and pretentious than 3w2s. While THREEs in general are not in touch with their feelings, 3w4s can very abruptly vacillate between tasks and deep feelings.

TRIAD

THREEs, along with TWOs and FOURs, are part of the Heart Triad, which means that they take in information from their emotional centers. While THREEs are often disconnected from their feelings, they still *have* feelings about everything they encounter, and their first response is an emotional one. THREEs still do think critically and are very prone to action, but it's in response to what they pick up on in their emotional centers. The Heart Triad is the most image-conscious of all three triads, with THREEs being the most image-conscious within the triad. THREEs pay constant attention to how they come across in every situation and go to great lengths to alter their image in a way that accomplishes their purposes.

Shame is also a motivator for the three types in the Heart Triad, and THREEs try to avoid this feeling of shame by doing whatever they can to gain the admiration and respect of others. They believe (consciously or subconsciously) that if they can impress the right people, then they can escape this sense of shame and worthlessness. These types also all experience themselves in relation to other people, for better or for worse.

STANCE

THREEs, along with SEVENs and EIGHTs, are in the Aggressive Stance. All three types are oriented against other people. THREEs see people as tasks to accomplish along the way of getting to where they want to go. This perspective can result in THREEs being very assertive and potentially bulldozing over other people. They know what they want, they know where they need to go, and they don't often let people get in their way. This stance can lead to THREEs having a hard time understanding the effect that they have on other people. THREEs are very forward-looking, and they always know what they need to do next to accomplish their goals. These types are also feeling-repressed, meaning that they do and think more consciously than they feel. Feelings get in the way of productivity and efficiency, so THREEs can compartmentalize and turn their feelings off to a given situation so that they can accomplish what they've set out to do. Being in the Heart Triad while also feeling repressed usually means that THREEs are asleep to their feelings, which actually carry much more weight than they'd like to admit.

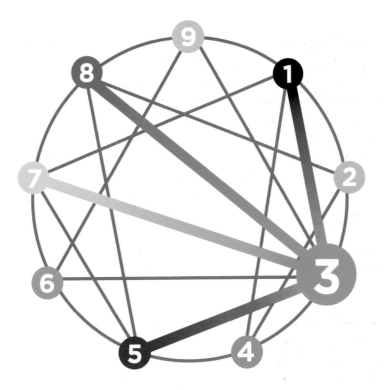

MISSED CONNECTIONS

Here are the "missed connections" for THREE:

»—→ **THREE and ONE:** THREEs and ONEs are united by their mutual drive for continuous improvement. They are literal, organized, practical, have a strong work ethic, and have a "holy discontent," or are rightly dissatisfied, with things that are merely adequate. Both types struggle with repressing emotions while at the same time feeling very deeply.

»—→ **THREE and FIVE:** These types are achievers. They see clearly and are smart, focused, diligent hard workers who can accomplish great things when they put their minds to work. They hate waste and love efficiency. More than anything, they are united by how disconnected they are (or can be) from their feelings and emotional selves.

»—→ **THREE and SEVEN:** Both are very forward-thinking types as members of the Aggressive Stance. Both types love adventure, are optimistic, are determined, and have the ability to reframe reality to meet their needs. They both are able to match the energy in the room and rally people together.

»—→ **THREE and EIGHT:** THREEs and EIGHTs are natural leaders, and you know when they walk into the room. Deep love for their people turns into action. They both make great champions of people under their care. Both types hate inefficiency in all of its forms: inefficiency of feelings and in situations where people get emotional and don't come to solutions.

If You Love a THREE

There's a good chance that there is at least one significant THREE in your life whom you have loved for some time. Here are five things to bear in mind about how to best care for the THREEs in your life.

»—→ **Be real and transparent with them.** THREEs often struggle with authenticity given the perceived expectations placed on them to be polished, successful, and accomplished. When you are honest, transparent, and vulnerable, it gives THREEs permission and space to do the same. If you show THREEs that you trust them with the more unpolished areas of your life, it normalizes this practice for them a little bit more every time. It is neither realistic nor fair to expect a THREE to take off some of their masks if you're not willing to take yours off as well.

»—→ **Don't put them on a pedestal.** THREEs are often accomplished, talented, and resourceful people. It can be easy for the rest of us to be envious of them because of how much we think they have it all together. Making comments around a THREE about how they are so perfect, successful, or great at everything they do is actually not helpful to THREEs. This only solidifies their felt expectation that they need to be better, and it disincentivizes them from being truly honest with themselves and with you. Remember that many THREEs come off this way because they feel like they *have* to do so in order to survive or find acceptance.

»—→ **Be very clear in both word and action that you won't abandon them.** A core fear of THREEs is that if they show any of their blemishes, people won't really love or accept them. Their constant shapeshifting to fit the need of the environment usually isn't mere vanity; rather, it's their way of pursuing belonging. Tell the THREEs in your life very clearly with your words that you love them and are with them and for them no matter what, and *show* them that you mean it. If they ever reach out for help or tell you that they are struggling with something, go the extra mile for them. Recognize how special it is that they are opening up to you, and hang onto that connection tightly.

»—→ **Give them plenty of space to try to articulate their emotions.** THREEs are pretty disconnected with their own emotions. However, this does not mean that THREEs are off the hook from dealing with their emotions. They still have to do the hard work of coming to terms with their emotions and emotional needs, but they may need your help. They need you to be patient if they have a hard time opening up. You may have to sit with them for a long time, ask the same question multiple times, or wait until they're ready. THREEs need space to come to terms with their emotions, and they need you to be persistent in your presence and patience with them.

»—→ **Pay attention to and affirm specific things that they do, including their effort.** THREEs put in enormous amounts of work in almost everything they do, usually because they feel the need to be seen as impressive and worthy of admiration. Paying attention to the effort that they put into anything shows them that you see them as they are. Affirming specific things really *shows* them that you appreciate them and that you're not just paying lip service. THREEs, when mature and self-aware, can accomplish tremendous things for the common good, and they will need all of the support and encouragement that they can get.

The Way Forward
UNLEARN THE NESTING LIES

Every single type has traps that they fall into when they are not aware of their internal narratives and motivations, and sometimes these can take the form of the lies that they believe about themselves and their place in the world around them. These lies end up becoming boxes that are built around us, and we need to hear and receive the truth that gets us out of these traps.

»—→ **LIE: It is not okay to be seen as flawed.** TRUTH: Having flaws only makes you human, just like everybody else. Your flaws don't define you, but they do serve as a reminder to the people around you that you are worthy of love, care, and compassion as well.

»—→ **LIE: I must be "on" at all times.** TRUTH: You are a human, not a machine. It is okay to rest, to not be achieving and winning people over, and to show people a less-polished version of yourself. You are loved anyway.

»—→ **LIE: People love me because of what I do, not because of who I am.** TRUTH: You are loved because of who you are, and nothing can change that.

»→ **LIE: There is nothing underneath all of these masks that I wear.** TRUTH: You have always been uniquely yourself, and *you* are what truly brings value, not all of the roles that you play.

»→ **LIE: I am what I do.** TRUTH: Just like everybody else you love, you're a person with needs, desires, gifts, a heart, and a soul, and that is just how you're supposed to be.

RIPPLE EFFECTS

Your actions and tendencies have an influence on more people than just you, and it's better for everyone when you pay attention to this influence.

»→ Just like how you don't want others to set you on a pedestal, you should remember that you can unintentionally place yourself there when you only project a spotless version of yourself to the world around you. Many THREEs often cut corners in work or other responsibilities, putting more effort into getting others to think that they're competent at something rather than actually doing the work to become competent at it. This pattern of cutting corners limits both you and the people around you, as you give people an incomplete picture of yourself and your capabilities. Everyone ends up dissatisfied in this situation.

»→ Remember that you limit others when you treat people like tasks. THREEs can easily fall into the trap of seeing people as tasks to accomplish in response to their self-imposed pressure to succeed. When you always prioritize task over relationship and production over the person, you inevitably cut the people in your life off of true connection with you. This habit leaves people feeling neglected, even when you don't intend for them to feel that way. As with any other type, limiting the people close to you is also limiting yourself.

»→ Pay attention to how you're seeing others as extensions of yourself. When you see your own sense of worth and accomplishment based off how accomplished the people close to you are, it places the same high expectations of success and efficiency on them that you have for yourself. This self-inflicted pressure is not ultimately helpful for you, and it is certainly not helpful for the people close to you either. Your own worth is not based on how successful you are, and it is most definitely not based on how successful your friends and family are.

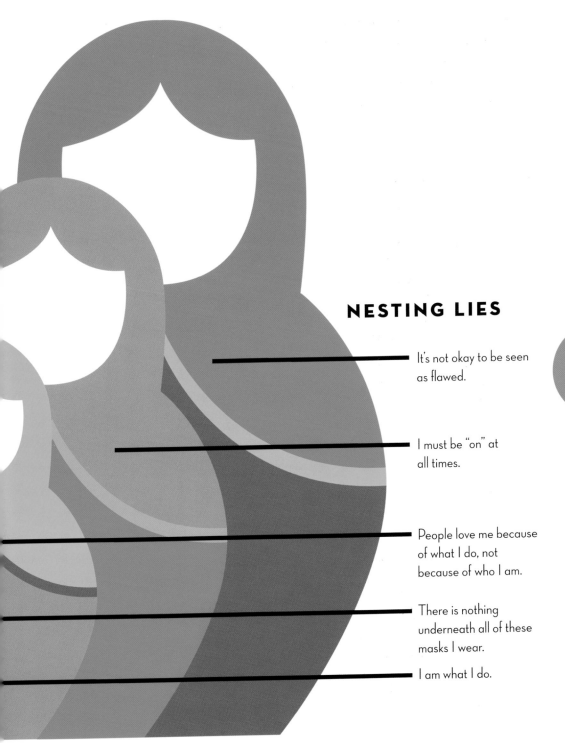

NESTING LIES

It's not okay to be seen as flawed.

I must be "on" at all times.

People love me because of what I do, not because of who I am.

There is nothing underneath all of these masks I wear.

I am what I do.

3

»→ **Reading Plans.** Being able to identify areas of growth or curiosity, finding books written by experts, setting goals and developing structures on how many to read and how quickly to get through them, and following through can all come very easily for THREEs. This practice allows you to be always exposing yourself to new perspectives and sharpening any given area of your life.

»→ **Silence.** In silence, THREEs will be forced to be self-critical and encounter their own dishonesty and compulsion to succeed. The key here is that THREEs must learn to face their shadow sides, failure, and defeats head-on rather than running away from them.

»→ **Sharing Vulnerably.** While vulnerability should be a practice for everybody, THREEs in particular should have a routine practice of sharing honestly and vulnerably with another person or group of people. This practice requires both self-examination and humility, both of which are threatening but so necessary if THREEs want to grow beyond their compulsions.

SELF-CARE FOR THREES

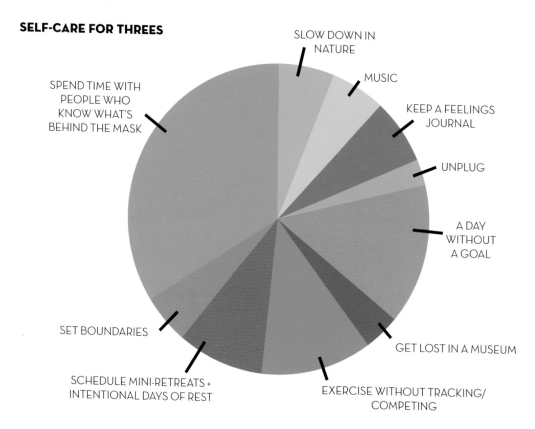

SLOW DOWN IN NATURE

MUSIC

SPEND TIME WITH PEOPLE WHO KNOW WHAT'S BEHIND THE MASK

KEEP A FEELINGS JOURNAL

UNPLUG

A DAY WITHOUT A GOAL

SET BOUNDARIES

GET LOST IN A MUSEUM

SCHEDULE MINI-RETREATS + INTENTIONAL DAYS OF REST

EXERCISE WITHOUT TRACKING/ COMPETING

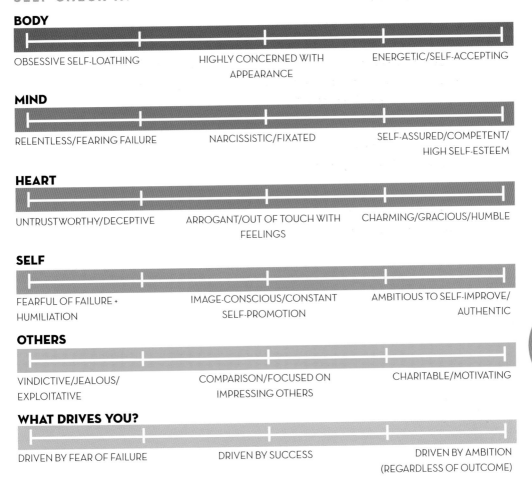

BODY

OBSESSIVE SELF-LOATHING | HIGHLY CONCERNED WITH APPEARANCE | ENERGETIC/SELF-ACCEPTING

MIND

RELENTLESS/FEARING FAILURE | NARCISSISTIC/FIXATED | SELF-ASSURED/COMPETENT/ HIGH SELF-ESTEEM

HEART

UNTRUSTWORTHY/DECEPTIVE | ARROGANT/OUT OF TOUCH WITH FEELINGS | CHARMING/GRACIOUS/HUMBLE

SELF

FEARFUL OF FAILURE + HUMILIATION | IMAGE-CONSCIOUS/CONSTANT SELF-PROMOTION | AMBITIOUS TO SELF-IMPROVE/ AUTHENTIC

OTHERS

VINDICTIVE/JEALOUS/ EXPLOITATIVE | COMPARISON/FOCUSED ON IMPRESSING OTHERS | CHARITABLE/MOTIVATING

WHAT DRIVES YOU?

DRIVEN BY FEAR OF FAILURE | DRIVEN BY SUCCESS | DRIVEN BY AMBITION (REGARDLESS OF OUTCOME)

The Reckoning

Many people need significant humbling encounters to break them of the unconscious compulsions that limit them and the people around them. THREEs are no exception. The reckoning for THREEs often involves some sort of public and/or prolonged sense of failure and not living up to their own expectations. Life is not a ladder full of rungs of successes and accomplishments that you can someday climb to the top. When the compulsion to see life and people in this way gets strong, you often need a reckoning of sorts to remind you of your own humanity and the humanity of others. Public or prolonged failure can soften you from seeing yourself as a machine whose sole purpose is to achieve. It can free you from the cruel pressure to perform all the time as you learn that there is life on the other side of failure.

FOUR

The Individualist / Romantic / Artist

The Enneagram FOUR is called the Individualist, the Romantic, or the Artist.

FOURs are creative, inspiring, witty romantics, deeply in tune with their imaginations and creativity. They are unique, paradoxical people: envious and empathetic, self-aware and insecure, great listeners and extremely withdrawn.

But by far their greatest superpower is that they are at the same time deeply sensitive and yet emotionally strong. These may seem to be opposites, but they are not to a FOUR. Unlike other types who may assign value judgments to negative or positive emotions, FOURs are skilled at fully experiencing all types of emotions without judgement: those that some might deem "good" or "positive" and also those that have been categorized "bad" or "negative."

Because of this, FOURs may have an unfounded reputation for being moody, dark, or morose, when in reality they just don't shy away from the inevitably dark parts of life. A crying FOUR doesn't want to be comforted and would hate to be told to cheer up, because cheering up would be inauthentic when life is sad. FOURs embody emotional strength when they bravely sit in the darkest emotions.

The challenge for the rest of us is to create hospitable space for our FOUR friends to be themselves without judgment or shame. When we learn to do that consistently, FOURs will feel safe enough to reveal their great gifts to a world that desperately needs to learn from their emotionally fluency.

DISCLAIMER

Even as we were preparing to write this book, we knew that the chapter on FOURs would be one of the (if not the most) challenging ones to write. The Enneagram FOUR is called the Individualist, the Romantic, or the Artist, and no matter which descriptor resonates most, at the core of the FOUR's identity is an extreme sense of individualism. FOURs believe they are truly unique in the world and that no test, book, or personality type will ever fully describe them. It is unlikely that a FOUR reading this chapter will be able to connect to all aspects of FOUR-ness, and that's okay. We know that not everything will resonate with every FOUR, but we hope that this chapter will be helpful for your community to better understand you in your FOUR-ness, as well as for you to better understand yourself even as it provides you with pathways for growth.

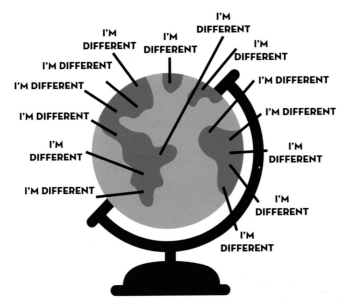

I'M DIFFERENT
I'M DIFFERENT
I'M DIFFERENT
I'M DIFFERENT
I'M DIFFERENT
I'M DIFFERENT
I'M DIFFERENT
I'M DIFFERENT
I'M DIFFERENT
I'M DIFFERENT
I'M DIFFERENT
I'M DIFFERENT
I'M DIFFERENT
I'M DIFFERENT
I'M DIFFERENT

A World of FOURs

The world would be a beautiful, curated, and emotionally intense place. There would be no more small talk, only truthful, deep, and meaningful conversations. Everyone would have great capacity to understand each other and would spend time empathizing with one another. Not much would get done, but everything would be processed. There would be great potential for people to be more connected but also great potential for tormented separation and loneliness as people competed for uniqueness and/or challenged each other's interpretation of authenticity. Regardless, a lot of melancholy art would be created, a lot of movies with sad endings would be artfully filmed, and a lot of angsty music would be written.

Motivation

Some of the motivations of FOURs appear externally. FOURs want to be their unique self and express this to the world. They may dress uniquely, wear their hair in a distinct style, decorate their work cubicle in a way that is countercultural, or even drive a colorful bike/car. In this way, FOURs stand out—not necessarily so that you will notice them, but so that they can express who they are. In other words, it's not for you, it's for them.

But below the surface, FOURs are also motivated by beauty. They want to make the world a more beautiful place and to find the beauty that others miss. FOURs can find beauty in death, sadness, loss, and grief and express beauty through creativity.

FOURs carry a lot of shame. They feel more broken, damaged, and deficient than everyone else. They tell themselves that no one will ever fully understand them and that no one will ever fully accept or love them. They are too broken to be fully known and fully loved and as such are deeply motivated by an internal sense that something is lacking.

The unofficial "poet laureate" of the Enneagram FOUR is most certainly Rainer Maria Rilke. Read his words below and you may hear the echo of the FOUR's inner narrative: thoughts of not fitting in fully, of wanting to connect and be fully found, and to be truly authentic.

I am much too alone in this world, yet not alone
enough
to truly consecrate the hour.
I am much too small in this world, yet not small
enough
to be to you just object and thing,
dark and smart.
I want my free will and want it accompanying
the path which leads to action;
and want during times that beg questions,
where something is up,
to be among those in the know,
or else be alone.

I want to mirror your image to its fullest perfection,
never be blind or too old
to uphold your weighty wavering reflection.
I want to unfold.
Nowhere I wish to stay crooked, bent;
for there I would be dishonest, untrue.
I want my conscience to be
true before you;
want to describe myself like a picture I observed
for a long time, one close up,
like a new word I learned and embraced,
like the everyday jug,
like my mother's face,
like a ship that carried me along
through the deadliest storm.

–Rainer Maria Rilke

The Shadow Side

The shadow side of the FOUR is marked by deep shame. FOURs are deeply afraid that who they truly are inside is not enough. Their unique way of expressing themselves is sometimes a coping mechanism, a way of overcompensating for the possibility that they may actually not be special. FOURs look around at the people in their lives and see others who are able to function in spite of their own brokenness, and they think that something must be missing in them. "Why is everyone else so happy and I am not?" "Why do they have what it takes and I don't?"

They are plagued by a nagging lie that tells them that they are too much for the world. In fact, they have probably been told throughout their lives that they *are* too much. In this way, FOURs have a lot in common with EIGHTs. But rather than reacting against this lie, FOURs lean into the lie, believing in their soul that they are too much for everyone and that no one will understand.

FOURs in Integration and Disintegration

It has been said that when we move toward different types in integration or disintegration, we make these movements because we need something from that type that we aren't able to get on our own.

FOURs who are doing well take on some of the best aspects of ONEs. They are able to be present, practical, and objective, no longer allowing their emotions to control them. They embody the virtue of equanimity and emotional balance, and they are able to express their emotions in a

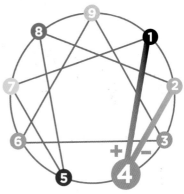

WARNING SIGNS

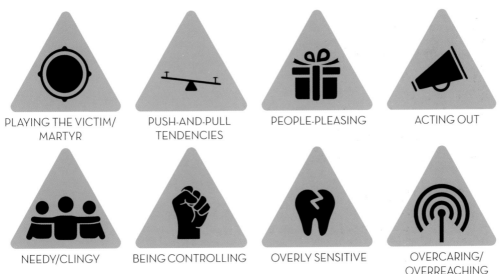

PLAYING THE VICTIM/
MARTYR

PUSH-AND-PULL
TENDENCIES

PEOPLE-PLEASING

ACTING OUT

NEEDY/CLINGY

BEING CONTROLLING

OVERLY SENSITIVE

OVERCARING/
OVERREACHING

deep, authentic way without their emotions getting in the way. In other words, they maintain their emotional fluency but are not enslaved to their emotions. Their emotional fluency begins to benefit others, as they are able to look outward and focus on the emotional states of others. FOURs in health, or mature FOURs, will be gentle, compassionate, empathetic listeners who are not self-absorbed or self-pitying.

Here is how our friend Alyssa describes integration:

> I'm able to be more rational and listen to my beliefs more than my emotions. . . I don't move from one extreme to another. Instead of going through emotional canyons and mountain ranges, I'm on a golf course which is mostly flat but has little inclines or declines (not even hills). I feel more sure in my convictions. I think through problems rather than feeling them out. I organize and make check lists and feel accomplished when I get things done. I actually make plans and stick to them.

In stress, FOURs will start to take on some of the unhealthy characteristics of TWOs. They may become jealous and envious of others who seem to have something they are missing. FOURs in this place may dwell too long in unproductive melancholy and self-loathing. In relationships, they may become overinvolved, clingy, and perhaps even codependent. Like unhealthy TWOs, FOURs who are not doing well may begin to keep a record of favors, manipulating others into loving them. They can be self-focused and condescending.

One way to gauge this is through the creative output of the FOUR. Whether their preferred creative outlet is cooking, baking, writing, painting, drawing, crafting, music, filmmaking, or something else, the FOUR in health will be able to set insecurity aside as they express the universal truths of the world in original art. The FOUR who is not doing well may be creatively blocked and repressed, or may simply be using creativity as a means to prolong or curate an emotional state.

Digging Deeper into FOURs
ENNEADICTIONARY: HELPFUL FOUR LANGUAGE

»→ **Equanimity (n.):** Equanimity is defined as emotional balance; emotional balance is the pathway to health for FOURs. Healthy FOURs embody this better than all other types, maintaining presence of mind amidst all emotional states. Unaware or unhealthy FOURs struggle with extreme emotions and suffer from a lack of emotional balance.

»—→ **Curating (v.):** FOURs are constantly curating their lives into a work of art. Memories are curated, external appearance is curated, home space is curated, and social media feeds are curated. Even emotions can be curated by watching that one movie, listening to that particular song, or returning to a certain place. FOURs are adept at curation.

»—→ **Paradox (n.):** FOURs are walking paradoxes, and their bent toward the extreme shows up in a variety of ways. They are known to employ the hot/cold treatment of others (a cycle of withdrawing and luring). FOURs may also vacillate between phases of exaggerated activity and phases where they are withdrawn and quasi-paralyzed. They are either all in or all out. There is no middle ground. Even the subtypes of FOURs vary greatly.

SUBTYPES

»—→ **Social (SO) FOUR:** SO FOURs suffer. They are emotionally sensitive and deeply connected to suffering, finding comfort in suffering and in expressing their suffering to others. They compare themselves to others and tend to see themselves as less worthy or lacking in some way. They have a deep desire to be understood for who they really are. They often doubt themselves, making comparisons to others and blaming themselves, triggering strong feelings of envy and shame.

4

»—→ **Self-Preservation (SP) FOUR:** SP FOURs are the countertype, meaning that they show up in the world less FOUR-like than SO and SX FOURs. They are not very dramatic or emotional and have learned to live with pain, suffering stoically by internalizing negative emotions. While they feel things deeply, they often have a "tough" or "sunny" exterior. SP FOURs are very sensitive yet may be private with their feelings or even disconnected from them. These FOURs may have a hard time identifying themselves as FOURs and may find themselves mistyping as THREEs, ONEs, or SEVENs.

»—→ **Sexual (SX) FOUR:** SX FOURs are intense, assertive, competitive, and vocal about their needs and feelings. They can appear aggressive to others, are demanding, and are not afraid to ask for what they need (or to complain when they don't get it). Their ability to express feelings of frustration, rejection, and anger may mask how sad or confused they really feel.

4W3   4W5

FOURs with a THREE wing (4w3) seem paradoxical. How could a type motivated by authenticity and emotional expression have a THREE wing marked by emotional illiteracy and deceit? These FOURs are more extroverted and image-conscious than other FOURs. They will likely be more ambitious and competitive as well. As a combination of two Heart types, they are more people-focused and more likely to struggle with deep shame.

FOURs with a FIVE wing (4w5) are truly unique types. To be a FOUR with a FIVE wing means to reach across the existential divide on the bottom of the Enneagram and bridge the gap between Head and Heart. 4w5s tend to be more rational, intellectual, observant, and reserved than 4w3s. As a combination of two Withdrawing types, 4w5s tend to be more introverted and withdrawn and have more of a head-heart connection.

TRIAD

All three types in the Heart Triad (TWO, THREE, and FOUR) take in information emotionally. They have feelings about everything they encounter. While every type has feelings, unless you are in the Heart Triad, body awareness or thinking will come first as you take in information, even if it is only for a split second. Outwardly, FOURs strike people as self-confident, happy, and harmonious, but inwardly they feel empty, incapable, sad, and ashamed. They are tuned into and experience themselves in relation to the feelings or behaviors of others. Alll three of these types struggle with feelings of worthlessness.

STANCE

FOURs, FIVEs, and NINEs are all in the Withdrawing Stance, meaning that they are oriented inwards and their identity and sense of self come from within. They meet their own needs internally and make decisions in the privacy of their own minds and hearts. FOURs live their interior life as if it were the real world and can often get lost in their imaginations, lacking the initiative to move their real life forward. As such, FOURs may have difficulty differentiating between the stories they tell themselves and the reality of the world around them. They are more oriented toward the past than other types, largely because no "doing" is needed in the past. They may replay conversations and scenarios many times in their heads, thinking about what they should have done or said differently. FOURs withdraw to protect their feelings and find their sense of personal value. They ruminate on relationships, conversations, and what is missing from their lives.

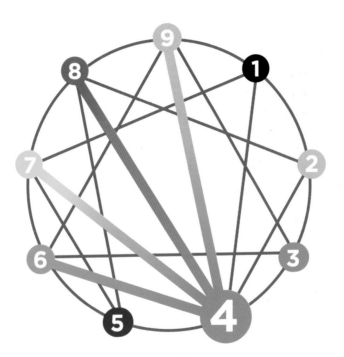

MISSED CONNECTIONS

Here are the "missed connections" for FOUR:

»→ **FOUR and SIX:** Both FOURs and SIXes are rebellious types and can appear self-contradictory at times. Both types are spiritually deep and deeply sensitive. Both types find fascination with the shadow self and the darker parts of life. They are drawn to dark stories.

»—→ **FOUR and SEVEN:** SEVENs and FOURs are seemingly opposites, but what they have deeply in common is that both types are motivated by deficiencies. Their passion for stories and flippant attitude mean that they are able to cultivate their external environments for certain emotions or aesthetics and can appreciate the mundane along with the sublime.

»—→ **FOUR and EIGHT:** Both FOURs and EIGHTs have been told that they are "too much" their entire lives, perhaps because both types are truly authentic. They are intense, emotionally vulnerable, volatile, inspiring, and gracious toward others.

»—→ **FOUR and NINE:** As members of the Withdrawing Stance, both FOURs and NINEs are oriented toward the past, which comes across for both of these types as nostalgia. Both types can identify with a sense of not fully belonging. As such, they may bend toward self-absorption and can come across as dramatic. Both types also love stories and reading, especially fantasy and fiction.

IF YOU LOVE A FOUR

FOURs are very misunderstood. It can be hard to know how to truly show and give love to some of the FOURs in your life. As we alluded to in the disclaimer earlier, there is so much diversity within the FOUR community, so you will have to be creative with the particular FOURs in your life. But we have done our best to compile some guidelines for how you can create safe space for your FOUR to be themselves without shame or misunderstanding. If you love a FOUR, here are a few things to keep in mind:

»—→ **Create safe space.** Author Henri Nouwen in *Reaching Out* defines hospitality this way: "Hospitality means primarily the creation of free space where the stranger can enter and become a friend instead of an enemy. Hospitality is not to change people, but to offer them space where change can take place." This is exceptionally true when it comes to your FOUR. FOURs need people who can take a posture of hospitality. FOURs also need a physical safe space where they can hunker down and be alone or be with people who understand them. Don't underestimate the value of safe space.

•• **The FOUR who is not doing well may be creatively blocked and repressed, or may simply be using creativity as a means to prolong or curate an emotional state.** ••

»→ **Slow down and learn to sit with them.** When your FOUR is upset, they do not want you to make them "feel better." This comes across to them as invalidating and condescending to the depth of their emotions. Instead, learn to sit with them in their emotions. Ask what they are feeling and take the time to listen to their detailed answer. Do not rush them. Realize that even a young FOUR is capable of emotional depth that many others simply cannot understand. Learn both *what* they are feeling and *how* they are giving themselves the space to feel it.

»→ **Reinforce relational security.** You may need to remind your FOUR again and again that you are here for them and you are not going anywhere. They fear that the people they open up to will abandon them. This does not mean that you should walk on eggshells around FOURs or in any way condone their hurtful behavior. But it does mean that you will need to go out of your way to reinforce the security of the relationship verbally and nonverbally. As our friend, poet Lisa Kay, wrote from the perspective of a FOUR, "Let me feel, let me breathe, and after it all, don't abandon me."

»→ **Use art.** FOURs are notorious for making connections between their emotional states and art in the form of poetry, song lyrics, music, visual art, films, books, or characters. The next time your FOUR is upset and you are having a hard time connecting, consider asking, "Is there a song that explains your feelings so I can understand better?" Let art be the medium that helps you find common language.

The Way Forward
UNLEARN THE NESTING LIES

Some of these lies are so entangled deep down in your FOUR soul, they may take a long time to unlearn. You may also want to write these truths in your own words, but here is something to help you get started. When these lies start to pop up, practice combating them with these reframing questions:

»→ **LIE: It's not okay to be too happy or functional.** TRUTH: This lie has a root in your past. When did you start believing that you could not be happy? That you could not show joy? Where is the objective, non-emotional truth in this?

»→ **LIE: Everyone else has it and I don't.** TRUTH: What do you have? What is it that you seek? Are you projecting onto others?

»→ **LIE: I'm an emotional mess and no one understands.** TRUTH: We are all beautifully broken people. While not *everyone* has proven to be a safe enough person to be allowed into your inner world, it's categorically untrue that "no one understands." Who has earned your trust? Who is just waiting to be let into your inner world?

»→ **LIE: If I am not special, I am not important.** TRUTH: Your significance has nothing to do with your efforts. You have objective value even when your subjective emotions are telling you otherwise. What is the goal of this authenticity you seek? Are you okay if people don't completely get you?

»→ **LIE: I am not enough.** TRUTH: Are you just afraid that someone *may* completely get you?

RIPPLE EFFECTS

The way you show up in the world has real impact on other people. Even if they may not tell you, even if you don't think you matter, even if you are alone, your presence does matter and has ripple effects on others.

»→ Every time you become enslaved to your emotional life, you forfeit functioning in the real life you have been given. Your emotional depth is a gift, but it is not an excuse to not "show up" to your real responsibilities. Despite your inner voice, you *do* actually matter in your life. The way you show up has very real impacts on people around you.

»→ Every time you believe the narrative in your head about people around you rather than reality, you are projecting your own misconceptions onto people who do not deserve them. When you sense this is happening, check in with your ONE side and speak objective truth into the situation. Journal your thoughts; don't project them.

»→ Every time you shut down to others, you are acting out of selfishness and not the generosity that you are so deeply wired for. Why do you expect that others will show up for you when you don't show up for them?

HEALTHY PRACTICES

»→ **Get in Your Body.** Get in your body with a walk, hot bath, or yoga. This practice will allow FOURs to connect heart and body in a meditative way.

»→ **Presence.** FOURs are withdrawn types. While it will be challenging, FOURs should practice mindfulness and presence to relearn how to tolerate overwhelming feelings without shutting down or isolating.

NESTING LIES

It's not okay to be too happy or functional.

Everyone else has it and I don't.

I'm an emotional mess and no one understands.

If I am not special, I am not important.

I am not enough.

4

- **Nature.** We once polled FOURs on our Instagram account, asking them what they like to do for exercise. The number one answer was that FOURs like to get outside and be in nature. Go for a walk with a friend, go for a hike, or sit outside and enjoy the unfettered beauty of nature.

- **Lament.** FOURs are wired toward the practice of lament. Using a journal, lean into your melancholy and write a poetic lament. Writing will allow you to lean into your imagination and process what you're feeling in a productive way that can be shared with others who want to understand how you're feeling.

- **Celebration.** On the flip side of lament, a practice that will be challenging (and necessary) is the practice of celebration. At the end of the week, write down five things that can be celebrated or five things you are thankful for.

- **Taking Time.** Non-FOURs who are reading this chapter might wonder what "taking time" means, but we bet that the FOURs reading this will completely understand. Linger, enjoy, delight in, and be present to the current moment.

SELF-CARE FOR FOURS

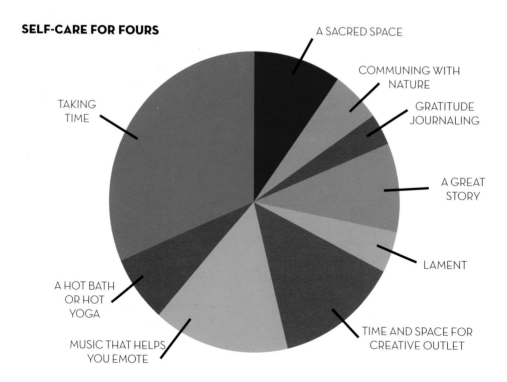

A SACRED SPACE

COMMUNING WITH NATURE

GRATITUDE JOURNALING

A GREAT STORY

LAMENT

TIME AND SPACE FOR CREATIVE OUTLET

MUSIC THAT HELPS YOU EMOTE

A HOT BATH OR HOT YOGA

TAKING TIME

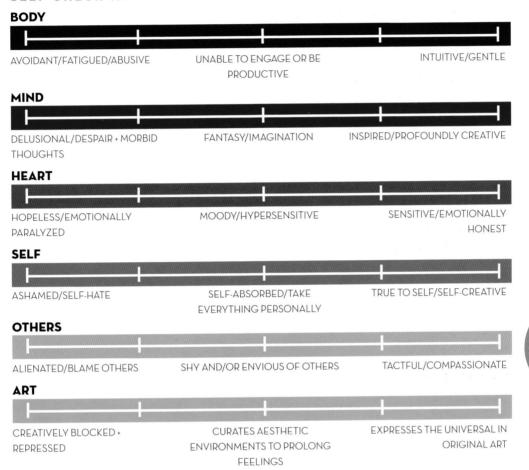

BODY

AVOIDANT/FATIGUED/ABUSIVE   UNABLE TO ENGAGE OR BE PRODUCTIVE   INTUITIVE/GENTLE

MIND

DELUSIONAL/DESPAIR + MORBID THOUGHTS   FANTASY/IMAGINATION   INSPIRED/PROFOUNDLY CREATIVE

HEART

HOPELESS/EMOTIONALLY PARALYZED   MOODY/HYPERSENSITIVE   SENSITIVE/EMOTIONALLY HONEST

SELF

ASHAMED/SELF-HATE   SELF-ABSORBED/TAKE EVERYTHING PERSONALLY   TRUE TO SELF/SELF-CREATIVE

OTHERS

ALIENATED/BLAME OTHERS   SHY AND/OR ENVIOUS OF OTHERS   TACTFUL/COMPASSIONATE

ART

CREATIVELY BLOCKED + REPRESSED   CURATES AESTHETIC ENVIRONMENTS TO PROLONG FEELINGS   EXPRESSES THE UNIVERSAL IN ORIGINAL ART

The Reckoning

If gone unchecked, a FOUR's tendency can be to let emotions control their life. It can look like a constantly increasing dissatisfaction with life until you are completely disconnected with reality. It can look like using the "push and pull" tendency with others so much that it breaks important relationships. It can look like deep and painful isolation that comes from never letting people in because they "don't understand."

FOURs have the opportunity to overcome these tendencies every day. This requires a lot of hard work, self-awareness, and humility. It requires sometimes going with the flow when it's best for the whole community. But above all, it requires that you be fully present in the real world, rather than in an idealized version of reality. As you grow in emotional intelligence and learn to speak the language of healthy emotions, you can find true understanding for yourself and others.

T Y P E

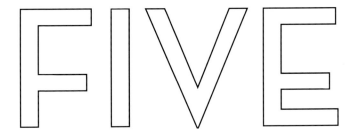

The Investigator / Observer / Theorist

The Enneagram FIVE is called the Investigator, the Observer, or the The-

orist. These people are curious, analytical, focused, perceptive, insightful learners. They are detached, highly boundaried, private, self-controlled individuals who spend a lot of time in their heads. The mind of a FIVE is like a castle: It is just as beautiful, cavernous, and abundant as it is guarded, private, and safe. In their mind castles, FIVEs turn the raw data they observe in the world around them into fair, wise, innovative solutions. FIVEs are good listeners, objective, and fiercely loyal people.

While on the outside FIVEs may seem to be emotionally steady, they are actually deeply sensitive. They prefer to keep their feelings private and to sort through them analytically and intellectually before they are willing to wade in and feel them.

A World of FIVEs

The world would be quieter—much quieter. Everyone would live their lives in their heads and would stick to themselves. At their best, people would be thoughtful, resourceful, and conscientious. But at their worst, the world would be made of stingy, skeptical people. Everyone would either be lost in thought or discussing the cool things they were learning. While people would be full of tact and respect for one another, they would also lack emotional expression, and the world's emotional intelligence would be low. While everyone would have studied how to get things done, no one would actually get anything done, so the world would be full of great ideas with zero execution.

Motivation

At their cores, FIVEs are motivated by their desire to be capable and competent. They are deeply curious people who have an insatiable thirst for knowledge. They want to understand everything about the world, about people, and about themselves, and they often obsess on a particular topic or area of study until they've exhausted their curiosity, at which point they will move on to a new topic. They are people who see. Often called the Observer or Investigator, FIVEs are constantly taking in information through their eyes. Unsurprisingly, many FIVEs wear glasses. The world is a playground for a FIVE's curiosity. They will likely never tire of exploring the reality of the world around them.

Beyond this motivation to understand, FIVEs are also fiercely independent individuals who desire independence from themselves and others. They want to remain largely undisturbed by others and to reduce their need for help from other people; therefore, they meet their own needs. They also believe that other people could do the same and may become frustrated when others cannot meet their own needs the way the FIVE can. They avoid neediness in themselves and others and want to avoid intruding on others' lives, as well as being intruded upon.

The Shadow Side

The shadow side of the FIVE is a deep fear. FIVEs are deeply afraid of being unprepared. They overlearn so that they won't ever have to appear ignorant; information makes them feel safe. Their fierce independence also reveals the complexity of their shadow side in that they are actually afraid that they won't have enough to give or that too much will be asked of them. They fear that others will invade their carefully constructed castle walls and find emptiness inside.

Nestled deep inside the FIVE's mind castle is a nagging lie that they are not capable. This lie is at the heart of the independence of FIVEs. Working so hard to overcompensate and prove to themselves and the world that they are actually capable, FIVEs learn to meet their own needs, believing that they can do everything on their own. They lie to themselves that they are strong enough on their own and don't need anyone else.

FIVEs in Integration and Disintegration

FIVEs live so much of their lives in their heads and can often neglect or merely forget their embodied selves and their feeling selves. Think of the absentminded professor who spends so much time in her laboratory that she forgets to eat meals. While others may look at this self-forgetting behavior as an unhealthy behavior or a sign of disintegration, disintegration for a FIVE actually looks very different.

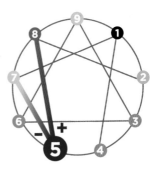

WARNING SIGNS

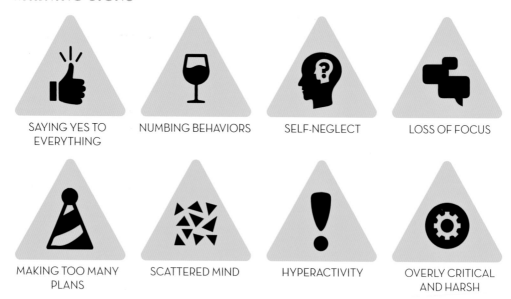

SAYING YES TO EVERYTHING

NUMBING BEHAVIORS

SELF-NEGLECT

LOSS OF FOCUS

MAKING TOO MANY PLANS

SCATTERED MIND

HYPERACTIVITY

OVERLY CRITICAL AND HARSH

It has been said that when we move toward different types in either integration or disintegration, we make these movements because we need something from that type that we aren't able to get on our own. Perhaps this is why, as FIVEs begin to disintegrate, they move toward SEVEN. If an average FIVE is boundaried, a disintegrated FIVE destroys their boundaries and lives unfettered.

In its extreme state, a FIVE who is very unhealthy and has been in disintegration for a long time may look very scattered, lose focus easily, and behave in hyperactive ways. They may make too many plans and say yes to everything, almost reacting completely against their normal world of boundaries and limits. They may take on some numbing behaviors, such as overdrinking, overeating, oversleeping, overspending, or overdoing it in general. FIVEs who have been doing their work and are self-aware may choose to let their guard down from time to time and indulge. SEVEN gives the FIVE something that they don't normally feel comfortable enough to indulge.

When FIVEs are fully integrated, they will cease to be merely a disembodied mind and will show up in their bodies, in their feelings, and in the world in productive ways. Theories will actually be brought to light and tested. Observations will be named and investigations will have results in the real world, not just in the theoretical world. FIVEs who are fully integrated move to EIGHT and look fully embodied as strong, capable leaders. Healthy FIVEs are self-confident, decisive, assertive, and active in the world. EIGHT gives the FIVE the integration they normally lack, and healthy FIVEs are able to take their brilliant insights and make something productive out of them.

Digging Deeper into FIVEs

»→ **Monastic (adj.):** FIVEs are wired for monastic life. They enjoy time alone and/or in their heads. They hate intrusiveness and intruders. Even their proclivity to emotional privacy and challenge with physical intimacy can lead to a celibate makeup in FIVEs. This makes intimate relationships challenging and long-term vulnerable, dependent relationships nearly impossible. It is both very costly and also incredibly healthy for the FIVE to take the huge risk of vulnerability and intimacy with another person.

»→ **Preflection (n.):** FIVEs think before they act, or instead of acting.

»→ **Collecting (v.):** All FIVEs are natural collectors of thoughts, ideas, knowledge, silence, and/or space. However, unhealthy or unaware FIVEs will not collect these things— they will hoard them. This is why, traditionally, the core vice of FIVEs is greed or avarice. FIVEs need to choose generosity over a scarcity mindset.

»→ **Manna (n.):** FIVEs run out of energy each day. Much like the Israelites in the desert in the biblical story, who only received a specific amount of manna (food) each day, FIVEs fear running out of energy and may spend much of their mental energy carefully choosing what and whom to spend their precious energy on.

»→ **Limitations (n.):** FIVEs operate in a world of limits and limitations. They create walls between head and heart, body and self (their mind), and between different aspects of their lives. FIVEs live very boundaried lives with many limits, both self-imposed and otherwise.

SUBTYPES

»→ **Social (SO) FIVE:** SO FIVEs pursue wisdom and knowledge, focusing on the big questions and becoming experts in areas that interest them. They enjoy connecting with others who share their intellectual curiosities, brilliance, and high ideas. Unlike other FIVEs, SO FIVEs are known for their generosity of intellect, energy, and enthusiasm around values and ideas.

»→ **Self-Preservation (SP) FIVE:** SP FIVEs are very protective of personal space and privacy. They set up a castle, a place of safety where they can ensure all their needs are met. They also focus on minimizing their needs in general. Often truly introverted, they set clear limits and boundaries and withdraw to their private castle when they want to be alone. Their boundaries extend to every area of life, and they find privacy and safety incredibly important.

5

»—→ **Sexual (SX) FIVE:** SX FIVEs are the countertype, meaning they show up in the world a little less FIVE-ish than the SP and SO FIVEs. They experience strong chemistry with one or two people but live an otherwise reserved life. SX FIVEs will risk dependence on their partner, and they are more in touch with their emotions inside, though they may not show them on the outside. They may test their partner's loyalty and resist sharing them with others. They idealize more, dream more, feel more, and therefore suffer more.

WINGS

5W4   5W6

FIVEs with a FOUR wing (5w4) are truly unique types. As FIVEs, they are deeply motivated by a desire to learn and understand, and they live much of their lives in their heads. But to have a FOUR wing is to reach across the existential divide on the bottom of the Enneagram and bridge the gap between head and heart. 5w4s tend to be more creative, and as a combination of two Withdrawn types, they may be more self-absorbed and isolating than other FIVEs.

FIVEs with a SIX wing (5w6) tend to be more extroverted than 5w4. As a combination of two head types, they are more anxious, skeptical, cautious, and scientific than 5w4. They are more people-focused, loyal, and dependent than other FIVEs.

TRIAD

All three types in the Head Triad (FIVE, SIX, and SEVEN) take in information analytically through their minds. Also called the Fear Triad, they have difficulty making decisions and planning for the future. FIVEs are afraid of doing something unreasonable or making a mistake. As such, they overlearn, overthink, and overanalyze.

STANCE

FIVEs are in the Withdrawing Stance, meaning they are oriented inward and their identity and sense of self come from within. They meet their own needs internally and make decisions in the privacy of their own minds and hearts. FIVEs live their interior life as if it were the real world and can often get lost in their mind castles, lacking the initiative to move their real life forward. They are more oriented toward the past than other types, largely because no "doing" is needed in the past. They may replay conversations and scenarios over many times in their heads, thinking about what they should have done or said differently.

FIVEs withdraw to process information and see withdrawing as a helpful stance to take in the world, as it helps them develop their own idea systems. As a part of the Head Triad, FIVEs will withdraw to find and protect their objectivity and mental clarity, something that they hold dear. FIVEs also withdraw to quell anxiety. In fact, FIVEs are the most withdrawn of all nine types.

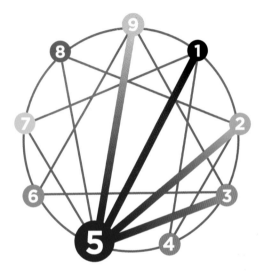

MISSED CONNECTIONS

Here are the "missed connections" for FIVE:

»—→ **FIVE and ONE:** Both ONEs and FIVEs are hardworking types with strong work ethics. They are dependable and reliable people. Neither will cut corners for the sake of time. Rules matter for them, and boundaries are encouraged.

»→ **FIVE and TWO:** At first glance, TWOs and FIVEs are complete opposites. TWOs are compulsive givers, and FIVEs are inclined to let them give. These two types often find each other early in life and partner up, believing that they have found their counterpart in the other. While this can be true, what these two types have in common is that they both struggle with asking for help when they are truly in a vulnerable place. Neither type wants to have to depend on others.

»→ **FIVE and THREE:** Both THREEs and FIVEs are achievers. They see clearly and are smart, focused, diligent hard workers who can accomplish great things when they put their minds to work. They hate waste and love efficiency. More than anything, they are united by how disconnected they are (or can be) from their feelings and emotional selves.

»→ **FIVE and NINE:** FIVEs and NINEs are both in the Withdrawing Stance and have strong avoidant tendencies. They are private, good listeners, hold the secrets of others, and create cognitive distance to stay "safe." Both types are perceptive deep thinkers who enjoy intellectually stimulating conversations and topics. Both types also value sleep—a lot.

If You Love a FIVE

Chances are that by now you have identified some FIVEs in your life. Just like with any of the nine types, there are many areas of potential conflict with FIVEs. It's likely that you had not understood just how boundaried the FIVEs in your life are. FIVEs likely have mental, emotional, and physical boundaries, as well as ones with their time and home, to name a few. So if you love a FIVE, here are five things to keep in mind:

»→ **The mind castle is real.** FIVEs are very comfortable in their heads. Their minds are very safe spaces, and they are able to sort through their feelings and experiences in their minds alone, without your help. This likely means that they are not verbal processors and may find verbal processing nearly impossible until they have done their work of sorting through information in their own head first. Please don't ask them to name their feelings and emotions without having the space to think first. And above all else, when a FIVE tells you how they feel, believe them—even if they are not displaying outward signs of the emotions they feel. By the time a FIVE is able to tell you how they feel, they have processed their hearts and know what they feel. Believe them.

»→ **They need a real-life castle too.** FIVEs need a safe physical space that is all theirs that they can trust will not get disrupted. If you live with a FIVE, make sure that they have a space where they can retreat to when the world gets too overwhelming. Do not disrupt their physical space. They will flourish as a person and in a relationship with you if they are able to maintain their own independent space.

»→ **Help them integrate.** FIVEs need to be reminded to get in their body. They will be better thinkers, better feelers, and better people in relation to you if they have a consistent physical practice that gets them into their body and out of their heads. When you notice the FIVE you love is getting too much in their head, encourage them to get in their body through running, biking, swimming, yoga, or some other physical practice.

»→ **Set clear expectations.** Many people don't like expectations, but FIVEs abhor unnamed expectations being placed on them. Be very clear about your expectations of the FIVE you love.

»→ **Offer help with no strings attached.** FIVEs take care of their own needs and minimize their own needs because they fear that once you get to know them, you will decide that their needs are "too much." As such, FIVEs have conditioned themselves to want to be around people who are just as independent and self-reliant as they are. If you take care of their needs for them, make sure they know you are doing it with no strings attached. You may find they will slowly let you into both their mind castle and their heart.

5

The bottom line is that you can love your FIVE well when you are clear and straightforward with your words, and when you are independent and not clingy.

The Way Forward
UNLEARN THE NESTING LIES

None of us exist in the world in a vacuum. As a FIVE, one of the core lies that you need to name and unlearn is that you don't need anyone else. Sadly, as a FIVE, you probably reinforce that lie every day as you prove that you are, in fact, a highly capable person who can meet their own needs. When these lies start to pop up, practice replacing them with these truths:

»→ **LIE: I am strong enough to not need anyone's help or comfort.** TRUTH: You are independent, but you still need other people in your life who can comfort you in ways you didn't know you needed, and who want to help you with no strings attached.

- »→ **LIE: I can't feel my emotions.** TRUTH: You access emotions differently than other people. Once you have the mental space to think your feelings, you will be able to feel them fully and completely.

- »→ **LIE: I can do everything on my own.** TRUTH: You are a very capable person, but you still cannot do everything on your own. Doing life with other people is what you were made for, and it's also more fun to take the journey together.

- »→ **LIE: People drain me, so I need to hoard.** TRUTH: Some people are very draining, but you have the wisdom and discernment to be able to name who is safe and who is not. You can give freely and generously to safe people without feeling depleted.

- »→ **LIE: I am not capable.** TRUTH: You are enough, today.

RIPPLE EFFECTS

The way you show up in the world has a real impact on other people. Even if they may not tell you, even if you don't think you matter, even if you are alone, your presence does matter and has ripple effects on others. While we are in no way advocating for anyone to sustain abuse of any kind, FIVEs are so extremely boundaried that they sometimes need to be reminded that the world is not a place of scarcity but rather one of abundance.

- »→ Every time you withdraw from a relationship or conversation because of the fear that the other person will be draining, you let fear win. A little bit of fear is a healthy motivator, but paralyzing fear that blocks you from relationships is damaging and harmful. Don't let fear win. Human connection is what you were made for; you just may need to be selective about whom you choose to connect with. Doubt your doubts.

- »→ Every time you are out of touch with your own emotions, you are at risk of causing negative ripple effects in the lives of those around you. Cultivate a practice of getting in touch with your emotional self, whether that's alone or with a counselor, spiritual director or guide, or other trusted person.

- »→ Every time you merely observe life, daydream about living, speaking, or acting, or have conversations in your head rather than with real people, you are not experiencing the fullness of life, and you miss out on what you were created for. Don't just be a passive observer of the world—participate in the world. We need your actions as well as your observations.

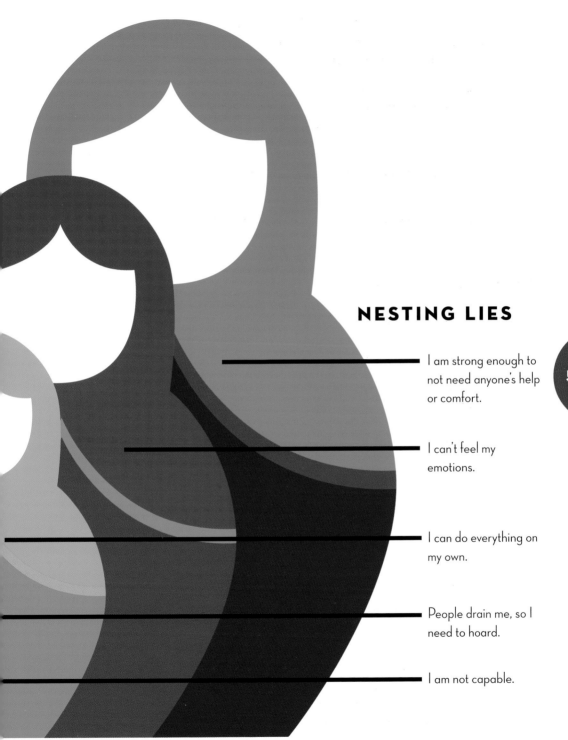

NESTING LIES

I am strong enough to not need anyone's help or comfort.

I can't feel my emotions.

I can do everything on my own.

People drain me, so I need to hoard.

I am not capable.

5

»→ **Service.** FIVEs are prone to disembodiment and disintegration, so it is important for FIVEs to get out of their heads to engage their hands and hearts. Regular acts of service or volunteering will provide the FIVE with a space to transform their whole self: mind, body, and heart. The act of serving others will also connect the FIVE with the rest of the world and remind them that individuals cannot be integrated as long as humanity is not integrated.

»→ **Generosity.** FIVEs prefer to withhold themselves, their ideas, and their resources. The practice of generosity will challenge and grow the FIVE. FIVEs should consider all of the ways they can share themselves and their resources. Where can you share your knowledge, wealth, ideas, and heart? Practice generosity in every way and by doing so unwrite some of the scarcity narratives you have been telling yourself for years. This will take time and practice but will be transformative for FIVEs. Trust that there is a well of abundance to be found, even if you fear you may run out.

»→ **Feeling.** Once you have identified an emotion that is inside you, give yourself the space to fully process it. But don't let processing be the end of your feeling. Feel the fullness of every feeling you identify. If you are feeling grief, walk directly through the grief without trying to get around it. Don't bypass your emotions—feel them, even if you feel them later or differently than those around you.

»→ **Presence.** FIVEs are the most withdrawn of all types. Therefore, it will be challenging but transformative for FIVEs to become present and learn to tolerate overwhelming feelings without shutting down or isolating. Practice mindfulness and presence; get in your body with a physical practice.

»→ **Boundaries.** Boundaries are good, but the boundaries FIVEs set up tend to be more like impermeable walls than the healthy boundaries that actually serve to protect us. Work to name which of your boundaries can have doors in them or can be turned into fences.

SELF-CARE FOR FIVES

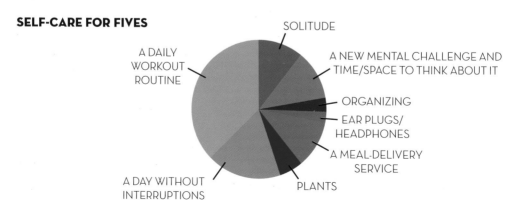

SOLITUDE

A DAILY WORKOUT ROUTINE

A NEW MENTAL CHALLENGE AND TIME/SPACE TO THINK ABOUT IT

ORGANIZING

EAR PLUGS/ HEADPHONES

A MEAL-DELIVERY SERVICE

A DAY WITHOUT INTERRUPTIONS

PLANTS

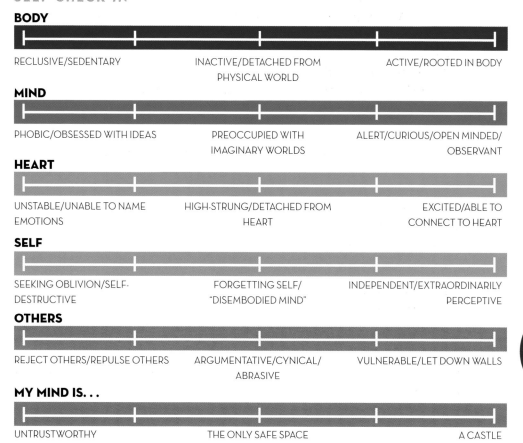

BODY

RECLUSIVE/SEDENTARY   INACTIVE/DETACHED FROM   ACTIVE/ROOTED IN BODY
PHYSICAL WORLD

MIND

PHOBIC/OBSESSED WITH IDEAS   PREOCCUPIED WITH   ALERT/CURIOUS/OPEN MINDED/
IMAGINARY WORLDS   OBSERVANT

HEART

UNSTABLE/UNABLE TO NAME   HIGH-STRUNG/DETACHED FROM   EXCITED/ABLE TO
EMOTIONS   HEART   CONNECT TO HEART

SELF

SEEKING OBLIVION/SELF-   FORGETTING SELF/   INDEPENDENT/EXTRAORDINARILY
DESTRUCTIVE   "DISEMBODIED MIND"   PERCEPTIVE

OTHERS

REJECT OTHERS/REPULSE OTHERS   ARGUMENTATIVE/CYNICAL/   VULNERABLE/LET DOWN WALLS
ABRASIVE

MY MIND IS. . .

UNTRUSTWORTHY   THE ONLY SAFE SPACE   A CASTLE

The Reckoning

Many people need significant humbling encounters to break them of their unconscious compulsions that limit them and the people around them. For FIVEs, this means it is crucial at some point that they experience deep loss and grief. Grief is an emotion you can't avoid. In grief, you no longer have the option of rationalizing everything, keeping intimacy at an arm's distance, and not participating in your own life. While there are many ways you can learn to be present with your emotions and body, only something as extreme and unavoidable as grief will jolt you into unlearning limiting compulsions. FIVEs should learn these lessons through some of the practices and self-discovery that we discuss earlier in this chapter. However, FIVEs are unlike other types in that the thing that most rapidly accelerates their reckoning isn't necessarily a character flaw. As you unlearn your tendencies quickly through grief or slowly through other practices, you will become a tenderized version of your former self, more present and generous with those around you and more aware of your own emotions.

T Y P E

SIX

The Loyalist / Skeptic / Guardian

An Enneagram SIX is known as the Loyalist, the Skeptic, or the Guardian.

They are faithful, dutiful, protective, cautious, thoughtful, vigilant, and reliable people. SIXes are people who are always aware of what could go wrong and spend a lot of time envisioning what the worst-case scenario could be. They are also highly prepared and resourceful people, because if the worst does happen, they want to be okay and they want you to be okay. SIXes are the people who listen to every word of the flight attendant's safety procedures; know where every emergency exit is located; and have snacks in case you get hungry, medicine in case you feel sick, and a charger in case your phone dies. This preparedness for whatever may happen is a superpower of sorts for SIXes; what comes very intuitively to them doesn't even cross the minds of many other people. Naturally, they are great protectors, friends, and companions.

While SIXes have an incredible natural ability to create security for themselves and others, many of their actions are rooted in fear and distrust. They believe that what can go wrong *will* go wrong, and they can't trust anyone who says otherwise. SIXes have a hard time trusting themselves because of their lack of confidence and acute awareness of their past mistakes. However, SIXes also have a hard time trusting others, especially unknown people in positions of authority, because they don't know if others are seeing or anticipating everything that they are seeing or anticipating. Their inability to trust themselves or others creates a constant tension that leads to unrest and the unsettling feeling that nobody is safe.

A World of SIXes

The world would be a very safe, planned out, predictable place without a lot of spontaneity. At their best, people would be responsible, welcoming, and peaceful, protecting each other and watching out for each other. The world would be an interconnected network, with everyone acting like a big support system for each other. However, at their worst, people would be anxious, fearful, overprotective, and worried. They would be too concerned with the future to act on it. Not much would get done, and progress would be limited.

Motivation

Each type deals with a certain compulsion that is their knee-jerk response to most situations, and for SIXes, that looks like a compulsion to be secure. SIXes see life as full of potential hiccups, problems, and threats, so they are always in search of people, structures, and routines that are safe and reliable. They are constantly scanning the horizon for any sign of danger or harm, even if it is miles away. The moment that a single red flag goes up, a SIX will then start to ask questions about every way that things could go wrong, imagine all sorts of scenarios, and begin thinking of ways to prepare themselves. SIXes who are unaware and running on autopilot take these red flags and quickly act on them, which can lead to others seeing them as frantic, insecure, and scared of everything. The scanning, preparing, and desire for security is what's going on underneath the surface. They want to have guidance, have the support of others, and make sure that everyone is being taken care of.

The Shadow Side

While the desire for security drives a lot of a SIX's behavior, it can also be the next-best thing that they settle for instead of real love. SIXes can mistake one's habits, patterns, and comfort, or the absence of danger or hostility, for being loved. It can be easy for a SIX to think that if you're there with them, nobody is mad, and nobody is in a dangerous or vulnerable situation; Everything is good. Being safe in relationships is a wonderful thing, and providing physical and emotional security for others is a remarkable gift that SIXes offer, but those abilities do not automatically equal love. The temptation of a SIX is to see safety and security as the end, rather than a means to the end.

These compulsions that SIXes face can result in recurring unhealthy chains of thought that hold them back from true growth and self-discovery. These thoughts include that they are never going to be okay, can't trust themselves, can't trust others, have to be prepared with plans and escape routes, will live in endless fear, and are going to be abandoned. Many SIXes have been shaped by an early exposure to the world being a scary place where bad things can unexpectedly happen. They have been let down by themselves, people in authority, external circumstances, and seemingly inconsequential events before, so they figure that it's best to always prepare in the event that happens again. All sorts of events can reinforce these fears for SIXes, which lead to a SIX's constant vigilance.

The "deadly sin" or vice for SIXes is fear—fear of danger, uncertainty, chaos, abandonment, not having their needs met, or being helpless or alone. Fear is a common feeling or experience among all types, but it holds particular weight for SIXes. How a SIX responds to fear is quite indicative of how healthy or unhealthy they are. When they are at their unhealthy extremes, fear does hold quite a lot of power in their lives. More commonly, however, it shows up in much smaller and more subtle ways. Fear can look like responding impulsively to any red flag that shows up rather than stopping to ask questions, constantly suspecting that people don't actually have your best interests at heart, taking strong measures to avoid danger (even if it is irrational and comes at a personal cost), or not being willing to extend the benefit of the doubt to people who are close to them. Fear in and of itself isn't inherently bad or unhealthy, but learning to respond to fear with healthy awareness is a constant battle for SIXes.

SIXes in Integration and Disintegration

When SIXes are in times of stress or disintegration, they take on some characteristics of THREEs. They can lose their grounding and succumb to their insecurities, often projecting their insecurities on others. This projecting can manifest as becoming more concerned with their own image or unhealthy competitiveness. They tend to numb their own anxiety by jumping from one task to another rather

WARNING SIGNS

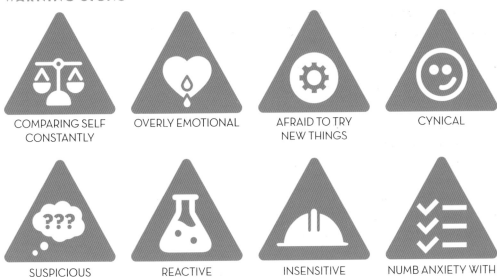

COMPARING SELF CONSTANTLY

OVERLY EMOTIONAL

AFRAID TO TRY NEW THINGS

CYNICAL

SUSPICIOUS

REACTIVE

INSENSITIVE

NUMB ANXIETY WITH ACTIVITY

than facing it directly. When SIXes are in stress, they can forsake their usual nature of thinking through everything and just respond impulsively to the environment around them. As with all of the other types, though, moving toward a different number in stress doesn't always have to be a bad thing. Sometimes if a SIX is thrown into a situation that they were entirely unprepared for, they can rely on this movement to THREE to get out of their own heads to be productive and simply do what needs to be done in a highly efficient manner. In these times, SIXes can ignore their Inner Committee and assert themselves more boldly than they usually might.

SIXes integrate to NINE in times of health. Healthy SIXes learn that it's all right to not be hypervigilant at all times. They embrace the ability to relax and trust that they and their people will still be okay. SIXes in health take on the positive NINE traits of being able to slow their minds down enough to deeply empathize with whomever is right in front of them. Much of a SIX's journey is the relentless pursuit of safety and security, and when they become more integrated, they learn how to rest and live in the peace and safety that they so desire. They rest when they learn how to trust themselves and the people around them. When SIXes learn to keep their hypervigilance at bay, they are then *most* capable of unifying people and communities, as they embody what it means to be an unanxious presence. A SIX who does their work to experience this integration offers the tangible security that SIXes provide combined with the internal harmony and tranquility that NINEs provide, and that is truly a gift to everyone around them.

Digging Deeper into SIXes
ENNEADICTIONARY: HELPFUL SIX LANGUAGE

»⟶ **Inner Committee (n.):** SIX minds are filled with the voices and opinions of trusted people, an Inner Committee. This Inner Committee is constantly debating and speaking, influencing the thoughts of the SIX and leading to analysis paralysis.

»⟶ **Analysis Paralysis (n.):** An inability to move forward on decisions because the SIX may not trust others' advice nor their own thoughts or opinions.

»⟶ **Worst-Case Scenario (n.):** SIXes have the capacity to put a negative spin on all situations. They may deal with fear in life with pessimism and worst-case scenario planning, often involving situations that would never cross the minds of other types. SIXes are always convinced that the worst case is a very real possibility.

»⟶ **Pretraumatic Stress Disorder (n.):** The "reliving of traumatic events" or episodes *before* the stressful situation ever takes place (if it even takes place at all).

»⟶ **Testing (v.):** SIXes will frequently test people in their lives, checking for loyalty and agreement as well as reassurance.

SUBTYPES

»⟶ **Self-Preservation (SP) SIX:** SP SIXes are cautious and loyal. They are highly practical and concerned with their own security in very tangible ways. The SP SIX is what is commonly known as the "phobic" SIX, meaning that they adapt to their fears and have many ways of hedging themselves against it, rather than displaying a more aggressive, combative approach. SP SIXes are the people who are always prepared for any situation. They can be more reserved and cautious than the other SIX subtypes, often taking a more subtle approach toward their circle of close people.

There is a commonly held position that the SIX is the only type on the Enneagram with two variants: phobic and counterphobic. While we agree that there is a distinction between SIXes who run toward their fears and those who conform to them, we disagree with the notion that there are two types of SIXes and only one of every other type. Rather, we propose that this distinction is best explained by the instinctual subtypes, because the three SIX subtypes are more distinct from each other than any other type's subtypes.

»—→ **Sexual (SX) SIX:** SX SIXes are commonly known as the "counterphobic" SIXes, meaning that while they are still motivated by fear, they can take a more aggressive approach toward their fear. They are more likely to run *at* their fear rather than running *away* from it. SX SIXes are the countertype, meaning they present as less SIX-ish than the other two subtypes. They are strong-willed, direct, and sometimes even seen as combative. They are bolder and more assertive than the other SIX subtypes, as well as more distrustful of people in positions of authority. They can easily mistype as an EIGHT or a ONE because of their bigger personalities that are seemingly unafraid to confront situations that they see as wrong.

»—→ **Social (SO) SIX:** SO SIXes are a combination of phobic and counterphobic. They are dutiful, precise, and more community-minded than the other SIX subtypes. SO SIXes can see things in a very black-and-white manner, which can lead to them mistyping as ONEs. An SO SIX always wants to make sure that everyone is on the same page about what is expected of each other. They like to have a hand in what's going on in the lives of their closest people so that those people will be there for them in their time of need. They are geared toward rules, order, and guidelines because of the clear expectations and reliability. SO SIXes are the people who adamantly stick to traditions among family and friends because to them, these traditions represent closeness and stability. Unlike the SX SIX, SO SIXes can find comfort in authority figures out of necessity.

6

WINGS

6W5   6W7

SIXes with a FIVE wing (6w5) tend to be more reserved, cautious, and cerebral. They are more likely to respond to fear or threats by dealing with them internally with lots of thinking, researching, and analyzing. They enjoy researching all sorts of things so that they can be prepared for whatever may come their way. 6w5s are usually more introverted and withdrawn than 6w7s.

SIXes with a SEVEN wing (6w7) tend to be more outgoing, energetic, and impulsive than 6w5s. When faced with fear or the unknown, they are more likely to move right into action than a 6w5 would be. They are lively, fun, and assertive. Their minds are highly active and productive.

TRIAD

SIXes are in the Head Triad, also known as the Fear Triad. They take in information through their thinking centers first, even if it's subconscious and instantaneous. SIXes spend a lot of time living in their heads, whether that is running through worst-case scenarios, preparing themselves for what may come next, or assessing security. They have very sharp and active minds, and their wheels are constantly spinning. The Head Triad is also known as the Fear Triad because they have a strong relationship with and response to fear. SIXes often dive headfirst into their fear. SIXes are more in touch with what they're afraid of and what could go wrong than any other type. This tendency does not mean that SIXes are afraid of everything, though. Their sensitivity to fear also gives SIXes an inclination to be daring, ambitious, and brave as a direct response to their own fear.

STANCE

SIXes are in the Dependent Stance. They are oriented toward other people and are dependent on others for their own security and identity, for better or worse. SIXes are also known as the Loyalist, as they have a strong tendency toward bringing people together and protecting those under their care. They only feel safe, secure, and well if their people are safe, secure, and well. SIXes feel the need to have people around them who are reliable, dependable, and understandable. Community is a very high value for many SIXes. SIXes can get into trouble with such dependence on others when they hold these high assumptions and expectations of others without communicating them, or when one person in their system fails them, they begin to project their suspicion on everyone else. The members of the Dependent Stance are also thinking-repressed, meaning that they feel and do before they think. This notion may seem a bit inconsistent with a SIX's location in the Head Triad. However, when SIXes are on autopilot, they can be quick to respond to feelings of fear or insecurity by jumping into defensive action without first stopping to think critically. It's in learning to pause and think critically before letting their worst-case scenario planning take over that SIXes find their growth and integration.

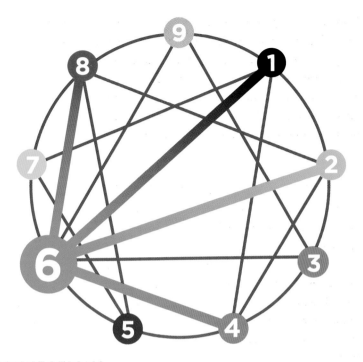

MISSED CONNECTIONS

Here are the "missed connections" for SIX:

»→ **SIX and ONE:** ONEs and SIXes both value "rightness." For both types, there is a proper way of doing things, and rules and hierarchy matter. They can easily come across as rigid and overprotective. Both types struggle with paranoia and self-doubt. They are both committed, reliable, and responsible, and they have a high value for others being consistent and dependable as well.

»→ **SIX and TWO:** Both types show up in the world in similar ways. They love people deeply and will do anything for their people. They are great at being present, and they are safe people to talk to. They love to have people around them and are great at building strong relationships. Both types consistently champion and care for others. They also both deal with insecurity in their relationships, often questioning how much people actually like them.

»→ **SIX and FOUR:** FOURs and SIXes are both rebellious types. They can appear self-contradictory at times. Both types are spiritually deep and deeply sensitive. They both find fascination with the shadow self and shadow parts of life and can easily get fixated on them. They are drawn to darker stories.

»→ **SIX and EIGHT:** EIGHTs and SIXes are both strong protectors and guardians. Their deep loyalty to their people can ignite the flames of their fire. You really want both types to be *for* you, and you really don't want either type to be against you. They both have a hard time trusting authority, and they have a sharp eye for seeing trouble coming from a mile away.

If You Love a SIX

There's a good chance that there is at least one significant SIX in your life whom you have loved for some time, but everything under the surface may come as a big surprise to you. SIXes, like everyone else, have their own set of particular things that mean the world to them, and these things may not come as naturally to everyone else. A wonderful part of the Enneagram is that it gives us the knowledge that shows us how to love people better. Here are five things to bear in mind about how to best care for the SIXes in your life.

Note that with SIXes in particular, their own human security systems hold a very special place in their lives, so all of these points are even more important if they're coming from an authoritative voice in their circle.

»→ **Show up—when you say you'll do something for them, actually do it.** SIXes are known for their loyalty and reliability. These characteristics are more intuitive to them than they are for most people. SIXes embody the sort of "ride or die" loyalty that all of us are lucky to have in our lives. Naturally, SIXes appreciate when their people are reliable and present when needed. So, if someone who is important to a SIX flakes on them and does not do what they said they would do, this would cause the SIX to feel hurt and sometimes betrayed because their own loyalty is unwavering. Flaking on a SIX can communicate that they're not a priority to you, which can lead to all sorts of other insecurities being triggered. It's good to be consistent with everybody, but especially so with the SIXes in your life.

»→ **Let them know that you're still with them.** It is of the utmost importance to SIXes who are close to you that you know that they are with you no matter what. Likewise, it's very important that *they* know that you are with them. SIXes are relational, community-minded people who see your well-being wrapped up in theirs. If you want to show a SIX that you love them, be clear in both word and action that you're with them, especially if they are not doing well or expressing concerns. This can look like a simple response to a text message, bringing them food, reaching out to see how they're doing, prioritizing time with them, telling them something about your day that made you think of them, or even simply telling them, "I'm here for you no matter what." SIXes can send out subtle or overt distress signals and see who responds to them, even in a very small way, as a means of making sure that their human security system is doing what it's supposed to do. Pay attention to this tendency and always be quick to respond, even if it's in a very small way. SIXes notice these small acts, and they appreciate them.

»→ **Validate their concerns.** Nobody likes to be belittled or dismissed, but much of the time, we can act like it's acceptable behavior when SIXes vocalize their concerns because we think that they're irrational. If a SIX expresses concern about something that you weren't anticipating, make them feel heard. Sometimes their concerns need to be teased out a little bit. Sometimes they need to be gently walked away from the edge of the cliff. Sometimes they simply need to be taken at their word without any questions asked. No matter what, take SIXes seriously and don't belittle them. See where they're coming from and make that clear. All of this is especially true when their concern is expressed on your behalf. They want you to be okay, and it is often their way of showing that they care.

»→ **Walk with them all the way through their concerns.** There are many instances when a SIX needs you to walk with them all the way through their fears and concerns. You can take it a step further by asking them what will happen even if it all goes wrong. Sometimes they need to be told and shown that even if everything goes terribly, they will still be okay and you will still be with them. Many times, SIXes feel like they are the only ones who hold their concerns and they will be all alone if their fears turn out to be true. Walk with them down this path and be perfectly clear that they'll still be okay.

The Way Forward

UNLEARN THE NESTING LIES

Every single type has traps they fall into when they are not aware of internal narratives and motivations, and sometimes these can take the form of the lies they believe about themselves and their place in the world around them. These lies end up becoming boxes that are built around us, and we need to hear and receive the truth that gets us out of these traps.

»→ **LIE: It's not okay to trust myself.** TRUTH: Your instincts, loyalties, relationships, and decisions have gotten you to where you are right now. You know what you're doing more than you give yourself credit for.

»→ **LIE: I always have to have a plan.** TRUTH: Sometimes life happens in ways that even you can't anticipate. Being unprepared only makes you human. Even if you don't have a plan, your sharp instincts will help you figure things out along the way.

- »→ **LIE: Endless fear controls me.** TRUTH: You have the choice to respond to fear in a healthy way. Fear may always be present, but you can have the final say.

- »→ **LIE: I'm not going to be okay.** TRUTH: While nothing in the future is ever guaranteed, if you have been okay by relying on yourself, your community, and the systems that sustain you, it is both reasonable and safe to trust that you'll be okay.

- »→ **LIE: I don't belong.** TRUTH: You provide desperately needed grounding, loyalty, and stability to relationships and communities. You are truly integral to every group to which you belong.

RIPPLE EFFECTS

Your actions and tendencies have an influence on more people than just you, and it's better for everyone when you pay attention to this influence.

- »→ Sometimes there are valid reasons to express doubt in a relationship. However, unfairly placed doubt can wear on the people in your life. Projecting your misplaced doubts on others communicates distrust, suspicion, and possibly misaligned expectations on whomever it is that you're doubting. If someone has given you no reason to doubt them and yet you are always putting their intentions into question, they become less incentivized to build trust with you. This process stunts your relationship, limiting both you and the other person. It is wise to exercise caution in this area.

- »→ Many SIXes harbor distrust because of how they have been let down in the past. Sometimes you are let down because of unreasonable expectations, but other times, your hurt is valid. While there are certainly relational hurts that warrant major distance and caution, holding on to smaller hurts and disappointments as evidence that someone will let you down again limits both them and you. At some point, holding on to past hurts gives the other person no space to grow at all, and life will become a series of self-fulfilling prophecies for you. You will inevitably let yourself down and be let down because nobody is perfect. The sooner that you release the people in your life from past hurts and disappointments, the sooner you will see your relationships grow in healthy ways.

NESTING LIES

It's not okay to trust myself.

I always have to have a plan.

Endless fear controls me.

I am not going to be okay.

I don't belong.

»—→ You have sharp eyes for trouble or things that can go wrong. This sharp eye is part of the gift that you offer communities that you're a part of. However, when you start to externalize and project every single worry that comes your way, you keep others at a distance from you. When you take a concern in one aspect of your life and project it on anyone who is listening to you, they now have to manage your insecurities and your problems when it's not theirs to manage in the first place. Learning the difference between sharing valid concerns and projecting insecurities will serve you and all of the people in your circles.

HEALTHY PRACTICES

»—→ **Memorials.** As people who are always scanning the horizon for what could go wrong, it's important as a SIX to have very tangible reminders of what has happened in the past and how you overcame life's difficulties. You are strong and resilient, and many of you have faced a lot of struggles to get to where you are now. Having some sort of memorial (it could be a token of sorts, a picture, or something you hang on your wall) to remind you of what you have been through and how you overcame can serve you in the future as you face whatever comes your way next.

»—→ **Mantras.** In a similar vein, having mantras or phrases that you can repeat to yourself over and over again can help center and ground you in what you know to be true, rather than what your fear or insecurity may be telling you. This process will look different for every SIX, but finding a phrase you know to be true and committing it to memory will help shape your thoughts whenever those red flags come up and fear starts to rise. This practice can lead to you seeing your fear for what it is, rather than having fear control you.

»—→ **Self-examination.** Asking yourself hard questions in response to fears that arise will also challenge your thinking and cause you to stop and reflect before you react. You can keep the worries and worst-case scenario planning at bay by responding to red flags with questions: Is this really true? Is it likely to happen? Do I need to be the one to fix it? Asking these questions is another important step in observing your own fears and worries rather than letting your life become dictated by them.

SELF-CARE FOR SIXES

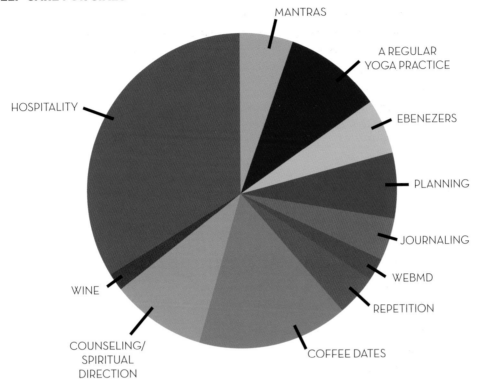

MANTRAS

A REGULAR
YOGA PRACTICE

HOSPITALITY

EBENEZERS

PLANNING

JOURNALING

WEBMD

REPETITION

WINE

COFFEE DATES

COUNSELING/
SPIRITUAL
DIRECTION

6

BODY

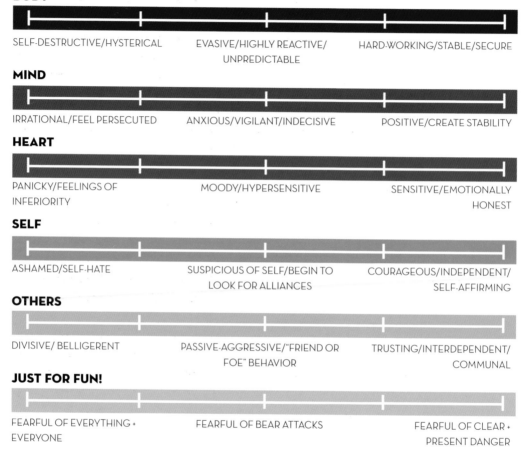

SELF-DESTRUCTIVE/HYSTERICAL   EVASIVE/HIGHLY REACTIVE/   HARD-WORKING/STABLE/SECURE
                                UNPREDICTABLE

MIND

IRRATIONAL/FEEL PERSECUTED   ANXIOUS/VIGILANT/INDECISIVE   POSITIVE/CREATE STABILITY

HEART

PANICKY/FEELINGS OF   MOODY/HYPERSENSITIVE   SENSITIVE/EMOTIONALLY
INFERIORITY   HONEST

SELF

ASHAMED/SELF-HATE   SUSPICIOUS OF SELF/BEGIN TO   COURAGEOUS/INDEPENDENT/
                      LOOK FOR ALLIANCES   SELF-AFFIRMING

OTHERS

DIVISIVE/ BELLIGERENT   PASSIVE-AGGRESSIVE/"FRIEND OR   TRUSTING/INTERDEPENDENT/
                         FOE" BEHAVIOR   COMMUNAL

JUST FOR FUN!

FEARFUL OF EVERYTHING +   FEARFUL OF BEAR ATTACKS   FEARFUL OF CLEAR +
EVERYONE   PRESENT DANGER

The Reckoning

Living according to compulsions can cause all sorts of problems in our own lives and relationships, regardless of what your type is. Many of us need to be broken of these compulsions in really drastic ways. This reckoning can take a few different forms for SIXes. It could possibly look like something bad happening to you or a loved one in a way nobody could possibly ever predict or anticipate. Perhaps it could look like taking every single precaution possible to prevent something from happening, yet it happens anyway. Sometimes it can look like insecurities taking such a hold of your life that you project and project until you push away everyone you care about. All of these scenarios involve learning the really hard way that you are not in control. You cannot save the world with your constant vigilance. Sometimes the way you try to hold on tight to the people you care about can actually drive them away. Whether you're prepared for it or not, life can be really hard.

The *good* news, however, is that life is always full of opportunities and small signs to learn these lessons without such a dramatic reckoning. We hope that as you learn about your own habits and patterns, you can become more aware of the influence that you have in your own life and the lives of the people around you. Starting with really small steps, you can begin to trust yourself and your people. If what you've feared has happened in the past, but you ended up more okay than you thought you would, why would the same not be true again? With fear comes the opportunity to exhibit the truest form of bravery—doing the very thing that scares you. As SIXes continue on this journey, you'll see that you can help others find their own courage too. The more that you embrace this courage, the more you will discover the safety that you seek and *become* that safety for your loved ones. As you become rooted and grounded and able to use your SIX "superpowers" for the service of others, you can learn to save the world by helping people stick together and helping them find their own courage. SIXes have braved the storms of life before, and you are capable of doing it again.

6

TYPE

SEVEN

The Enthusiast / Optimist / Epicurean

WAY OUT

The Enneagram SEVEN is called the Enthusiast, the Optimist, or the Epi-
curean. Chances are you know a SEVEN and you *love* to be around that SEVEN. Externally, these types are the life of the party; they are fun, entertaining, uninhibited, upbeat people. They exude joy and emanate positivity. Always up for an adventure, these types are going, going, going all the time. When emotionally healthy, they are engaging storytellers: curious, spontaneous, optimistic, talkative, thoughtful, passionate, celebratory, and active.

It may be surprising to learn that SEVENs are actually head types. SEVENs operate from their heads, thinking and planning constantly so as to maximize every day and moment for optimal enjoyment. If we could open up the mind of a SEVEN, we would find that they are constantly taking in information, learning, thinking, and processing. Just ask your favorite SEVEN sometime what they are currently thinking and dreaming about, and you will be ushered into a magical thought world unlike any other. The challenge is for the SEVEN to channel all of their mental gymnastics into a focused direction and to channel all of their knowledge into wisdom for the benefit of others.

But being a head type is more than just thinking, planning, and dreaming. SEVENs are master rationalizers, storytellers, and mental reframers. They can turn any negative into a positive situation simply by reframing their perspective. Think of reframing like a superpower: It is a gift that can be used for great good or for great destruction. Boring, tedious tasks and lists in the hands of a SEVEN can be turned into a series of engaging metaphors and images that help animate people. But as pain-avoidant types, SEVENs also use mental tricks like reframing and rationalizing to avoid the inevitable pain of life.

It is crucial that at some point along their journey, the SEVEN realizes that suffering is a part of life and they must make space for it. It can't be dealt with through mental reframing; it must be walked through. More than other types, it will be easy to tell the difference between a SEVEN who has been through real suffering and has come out on the other side as the embodiment of sobriety and satisfaction, and the SEVEN who has yet to address pain and suffering. The SEVEN who has made space for suffering will still embody all of the fun aspects of SEVEN-ness, but from a place of serenity and peace.

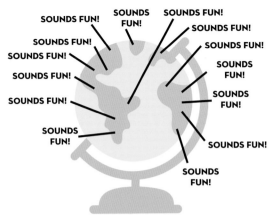

SOUNDS FUN! SOUNDS FUN! SOUNDS FUN! SOUNDS FUN! SOUNDS FUN! SOUNDS FUN! SOUNDS FUN! SOUNDS FUN! SOUNDS FUN! SOUNDS FUN! SOUNDS FUN! SOUNDS FUN! SOUNDS FUN! SOUNDS FUN!

A World of SEVENs

The world would be like an unstructured playground, full of possibilities and exclamation points! Everyone would make jokes, plans, and have the most amount of fun possible. Every day would be a big party, just because. However, all of the parties would be masking emotional emptiness and the fact that no one is ever truly feeling good. There would be long lists of brilliant, grand ideas with little follow-through. The world would thrive on turnover. People would change careers every year, and the best resumes would be the longest ones. Life would be frenzied and exhausting.

Motivation

SEVENs are called the Enthusiast and Optimist for a reason: They actually want to be happy and satisfied. They are motivated by joy and want to enjoy life, try new things, and avoid boredom.

While the motivations mentioned above are likely more visible and obvious to SEVENs and those who love SEVENs, there is much more motivating the SEVEN below the surface. SEVENs keep moving because they don't want to be tied down. They want to keep their options open and are motivated by the fear of being trapped. They want to escape internal anxiety, and they fear pain in all forms: being in pain, inflicting pain, and seeing pain.

The Shadow Side

The shadow side of the SEVEN is a deep fear. This fear can manifest itself in many ways: fear of stability, contentment, routines, happiness, or settling down. But at its core, all of these masks are covering up a deep fear of pain. SEVENs build a life of coping mechanisms to help them avoid pain.

Sometimes SEVENs will work so hard to avoid pain and fill their endless hunger for thrills that they will seek to fill the void inside with numbing behaviors. SEVENs are addictive types, prone to indulge by overeating, overshopping, overpartying, overdrinking, overexercising, and/or overscheduling themselves. Sometimes these indulgences will lead to very serious addictions, substance-abuse problems, financial ruin, and extreme anxiety.

SEVENs in Integration and Disintegration

When we move toward different types in either integration or disintegration, we make these movements because we need something from that type that we aren't able to get on our own. Perhaps this is why, as SEVENs begin to integrate, they move toward FIVE. The virtue of FIVE-ness is temperance—moderation, restraint, and abstinence. When SEVENs are fully integrated, they will be able to find a balance

between indulgence and sobriety, joy and sorrow, going out and staying in. In this movement of integration toward FIVE, SEVENs are able to quiet their bodies and minds and be fully present in all experiences rather than only looking ahead to what's next. You may notice your SEVEN is calmer, more creative, and more connected to their complicated inner world.

When SEVENs are not doing well, they disintegrate and take on some of the unhealthy characteristics of ONEs. They become visibly angry and critical. They may try to escape their own world by focusing on and blaming others. They may micromanage, become stubborn and unable to compromise, and pick on others. Rather than understanding their own needs, they turn outwards and may feel the "right" to tear other people and systems apart.

Many SEVENs note that disintegration comes with inner anxiety and that they will work harder to distract themselves from their inner world by creating order. This may look like anything from list making to obsessively cleaning their outer world in order to avoid the feeling of inner chaos. A SEVEN who has been in disintegration for a long time may only surround themselves with surface relationships, because anything deeper would be too "real" and therefore too painful.

WARNING SIGNS

UNABLE TO
COMPROMISE

PICKING ON/FIXING
OTHERS

OBSESSING ON
DETAILS

CHILDLIKE BEHAVIOR
MICROMANAGING

MICROMANAGING

BLAMING OTHERS

LACK OF MOTIVATION

TOO MANY
INDULGENCES

Digging Deeper into SEVENs

»→ **Escape Hatch (n.):** SEVENs like to have a way out of any situation. SEVENs are very forward-thinking and are always dreaming about what's next. The escape hatch could be something tangible, but it could also be a means of escaping into their own minds and finding freedom in daydreaming. SEVENs don't want to feel trapped, so their escape hatch is a coping mechanism that addresses this deep desire.

»→ **Reframing (v.):** SEVENs are masters at taking any situation that is too sad, too heavy, or too negative and reframing it in a more positive light. It is almost second nature for SEVENs to reframe and find the silver lining in any situation. This can be either conscious or unconscious.

»→ **FOMO (n.):** No other type embodies the fear of missing out (FOMO) than SEVENs. They are the early adopters of the Enneagram. SEVENs want to do it all, so staying present in the moment and being content with just one place is a challenge for SEVENs.

SUBTYPES

»→ **Social (SO) SEVEN:** SO SEVENs are the countertype, meaning they are more generous and service-minded than other SEVENs, acting with temperance. They want to avoid being seen as self-interested and focus on sacrificing their own desires to serve others instead. They are socially responsible, generous, and will sacrifice their own needs to ease others' suffering. They are judgmental toward selfishness. SO SEVENs are very TWO-like in the way they show up in the world.

»→ **Self-Preservation (SP) SEVEN:** SP SEVENs are great networkers who want the best for everyone. They are very practical, talkative, amiable, and good at getting what they want. They gather a close community of supporters. They are opportunistic, self-interested, and seek pleasure. They are also good at rationalizing and defending their actions/desires.

»→ **Sexual (SX) SEVEN:** SX SEVENs are dreamers, idealists, and romantics. They imagine something better than their everyday reality, seeing the world through rose-colored glasses and seeing the potential in everything. They sometimes see things as they could be or how they imagine them to be, rather than how things actually are. They may dislike the predictable and seem unrealistic or naive in their positivity.

7

7W6   **7W8**

SEVENs with a SIX wing (7w6) are an interesting blend of "optimism" and "pessimism." These types tend to be responsible, childlike, playful, relationship-oriented, anxious, and outgoing. They are more others-focused and find themselves bound in loyalty in ways that other SEVENs may not.

SEVENs with an EIGHT wing (7w8) are truly unique types. As a blend of two aggressive types, they are more adventurous, strong, passionate, intense, creative, quick, and bold than other SEVENs. Our friend, Brandon, a 7w8, prefers to describe himself as a "SEVEN and a half," because of how strongly the influence of EIGHT is on the SEVEN-ness of a 7w8. These types are SEVENs at their core but have EIGHT-like loyalty and rage and a strong desire to protect people.

TRIAD

As a part of the Head Triad, SEVENs take in information analytically, through their minds. The Head Triad is also called the Fear Triad; fear is a motivator for all three types. For SEVENs, this means that they deal with fear by rationalizing at all times. SEVENs are known as optimists, though a more accurate way to understand their optimism is that optimism is one of the coping mechanisms SEVENs have formed to deal with the world.

STANCE

SEVENS are in the Aggressive Stance, meaning that they are oriented outwards against others and are assertive (or aggressive) in naming their needs and seeing them met. They know what they want, they know where they want to go, and they will go there, not allowing things or people to stand in their way.

Aggressive types are oriented toward the future rather than the present or past, believing nothing will happen in the future unless they make it happen. A SEVEN's mental space is very much focused on the future and on what's next. The dreams of SEVENs are very important to them, possibly even confused with their needs and wants. SEVENs will likely pursue all three of these things (dreams, needs, and wants) with the same urgency, unable to differentiate between or prioritize which is which, and they will run after all three until their needs are met.

SEVENs may find it hard to fully get in touch with their feelings, leading to them being labeled "feeling-repressed." SEVENs do and think more than they feel and are more dismissive of feelings in general. As feelings are not readily available in their own lives, they may struggle to make space for the feelings of others, not because they are intentionally being dismissive, but merely because feelings are not on their radar. SEVENs often express their feelings for others in indirect ways through notes, gifts, and texts.

MISSED CONNECTIONS

Here are the missed connections for SEVEN:

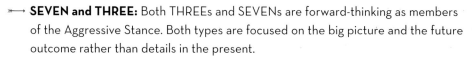

»→ **SEVEN and TWO:** Both TWOs and SEVENs are very open to the world. They show up in a childlike way: SEVENs have a childlike joy and lightness, and TWOs can tend toward a childlike dependence in relationships. Both types struggle with serious FOMO and are adept at curating social experiences.

»→ **SEVEN and THREE:** Both THREEs and SEVENs are forward-thinking as members of the Aggressive Stance. Both types are focused on the big picture and the future outcome rather than details in the present.

»→ **SEVEN and FOUR:** At first glance, SEVENs and FOURs are seemingly opposites, but both types are motivated by deficiencies—they just respond in very different ways. Their deep passion for stories and IDGAF attitude mean that they are able to cultivate their external environments for certain emotions/aesthetics and can appreciate the mundane along with the sublime.

»→ **SEVEN and NINE:** NINEs and SEVENs don't look like they have a lot in common on the surface, but both types are extremely pain avoidant. They're both funny, fun-loving, generous, versatile, and adaptable types, ready to go with the flow. Both types can also come across as distractible or scattered.

If You Love a SEVEN

By now, you have named some SEVENs in your life. If you love a SEVEN, here are some things to keep in mind:

»→ **Big ideas trump details.** When a SEVEN presents a new idea to you, let them get the whole idea out before you attack the details. Don't rush to the end or stress out over how things will be accomplished. Typos and mistakes on first drafts won't bother the SEVEN who can already see the future finished work, and pointing them out too soon may kill their enthusiasm.

»→ **Create safe space for dreams.** SEVENs need to dream and are usually very excited to talk about their latest dream. Rather than minimizing their dreams, ask leading questions like "What will happen if this dream becomes reality?" or "What will it feel like to be in this future space?"

»→ **They are more than the life of the party.** Stop asking SEVENs to always be the life of the party, but respect them when they want to fill that role. Examine your relationships with the SEVENs in your life. Are you expecting them to bear too much social weight? Carry the boring meeting? Reframe their (or your) anxiety?

»→ **SEVENs are different, not deficient.** Just because some SEVENs struggle with consistent communication doesn't mean they don't love you. Similarly, just because it can be harder for a SEVEN to get in touch with their heart doesn't mean they don't have one. Look for ways that your SEVEN is indirectly communicate their feelings to you.

The bottom line is that you can love your SEVEN well when you give them space, encouragement, and social energy to be the fullness of who they are in all of their complicated awesomeness.

The Way Forward
UNLEARN THE NESTING LIES

As a SEVEN, one of the core lies that you need to name and unlearn is that you don't have enough and that you will never have enough. When these lies start to pop up, challenge them with these questions and truths:

»→ **LIE: It's not okay to settle down, be content, or find stability.**
TRUTH: Use your brilliant mind to reframe this lie. What will happen if you find a routine that actually works for you? What if you meet a person who you makes you feel as though life without them would be more of a trap than life together? What if stability gives you peace and serenity?

»→ **LIE: I always have to be the life of the party.**
TRUTH: Where is this lie coming from? Does it stem from within that you are nothing, and have nothing to offer, if you are *not* the life of the party? Or does it come from others' expectations on you?

NESTING LIES

It's not okay to settle down, be content, or find stability.

I always have to be the life of the party.

I can't handle negative feelings.

I can't miss out.

I am empty.

»—→ **LIE: I can't handle negative feelings.** TRUTH: As a part of the Aggressive Stance, you have a tendency to minimize feelings in general, and the idea that some feelings are negative and others are positive is really a misnomer. All feelings are healthy, and we need to learn to be aware of them. You can't avoid the dark parts of life, like grief. You have to walk through them.

»—→ **LIE: I can't miss out.** TRUTH: FOMO is really just a state of heightened anxiety. Whenever you feel this lie creeping up, take a moment and remind yourself what you value in life, whether that is family, friends, work, security, health, or something else. Wouldn't "missing out" on these things be the real FOMO? In relation to what you value most, what does it really matter if you skip one party or event?

»—→ **LIE: I am empty.** TRUTH: You are far from empty; you are abundantly full. You have a brilliant mind that is full of rich ideas and dreams and a passion for life that others are envious of.

RIPPLE EFFECTS

The way you show up in the world has real impact on other people. Even if they may not tell you, even if you don't think you matter, even if you are alone, your presence does matter and has ripple effects on others. As a SEVEN, you are more wired to not see these ripple effects than other people.

»—→ Every time you write people off rather than treating them as the precious people they are, you are sending the message that they are disposable.

»—→ Every time you give in to indulgent, addictive behavior in an attempt to escape reality, you dig yourself deeper into a hole of dissatisfaction. Reality will be harder to satisfy as long as you distance yourself from it.

»—→ Every time you quit, never sticking with anything/anyone long enough to get beyond the surface and into the real heart of things, you send the message that you don't care about others. Stay committed even after the honeymoon phase is over.

HEALTHY PRACTICES

»—→ **Solitude.** As a SEVEN, you may not *want* to be alone, but older, wiser SEVENs tell us that scheduling alone time and sticking to it are key tools for integration. Start small with a short amount of solitude each day, or one longer amount each week, and stick to it.

»→ **Wonder.** Slowing down isn't easy for energetic, boisterous SEVENs. But all SEVENs are blessed with a childlike approach to the world that will make you a good candidate for practicing wonder. Practicing wonder means to notice and be attuned to the present moment, to see what is good and life-giving now, rather than what could be life-giving in the future. Wonder is the adventure of the present moment, not the next best thing.

»→ **Fasting/Sacrifice.** Fasting will be a challenging practice for SEVENs, who are much more geared toward indulgence and celebration. This practice will help you as a SEVEN not to remain addicted to experiences. Counter your default practice of indulgent behavior with one of abstinence. If you are new to this practice, start by giving up something for someone you love—give purpose to your sacrifice.

»→ **Challenge Your Tendencies.** Over the course of a week, make a list of all of the moments where you lifted a room and then ask yourself these questions: Why did you do it? What was the cost? What truths are you helping people (or yourself) avoid by acting like the life of the party? Use this practice to check in with some of your autopilot responses.

SELF-CARE FOR SEVENS

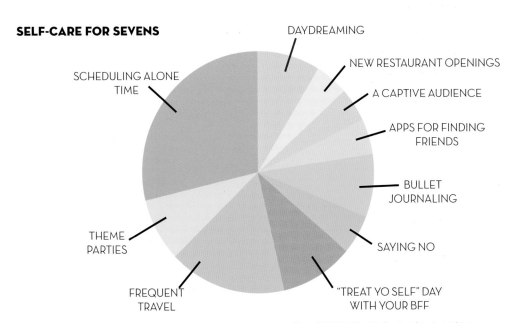

DAYDREAMING

NEW RESTAURANT OPENINGS

SCHEDULING ALONE TIME

A CAPTIVE AUDIENCE

APPS FOR FINDING FRIENDS

BULLET JOURNALING

THEME PARTIES

SAYING NO

FREQUENT TRAVEL

"TREAT YO SELF" DAY WITH YOUR BFF

BODY

NO ENERGY/BINGEING   IN PERPETUAL MOTION   VIVACIOUS/ENERGETIC
(DOING TOO MANY THINGS)

MIND

ESCAPISM/DESPAIR   SEEKING NEW THINGS/   FIND EVERYTHING INVIGORATING
FEAR OF BEING BORED

HEART

ERRATIC MOOD SWINGS   UNABLE TO KNOW WANTS + NEEDS   GRATEFUL/JOYOUS/CHEERFUL

SELF

IMPULSIVE/NOT DEALING WITH   SELF-CENTERED/UNINHIBITED   RESILIENT/EAGER/SPONTANEOUS
ANXIETY

OTHERS

DEMANDING/PUSHY/INSENSITIVE   PERFORMING/WISE-CRACKING/   RESPONSIVE/ATTENTIVE/
FLAMBOYANT   UNIFYING

MY TO-DO LIST IS. . .

MANY ITEMS, NONE COMPLETED   MANY ITEMS, SOME COMPLETED   FINISHED ONE THING BEFORE
MOVING ON

The Reckoning

The reckoning for a SEVEN will likely be centered on suffering, something so big that it cannot be avoided. You must come to grips with the fact that suffering is a part of life and must make space for it.

> **Suffering is a part of life and you must make space for it.**

A grief counselor once advised that the only way to deal with suffering is to go directly through the middle of the cloud. And this is the lesson for the SEVENs who finds themselves in one of life's inevitable dark times. You *must* develop skills to help you walk directly through the middle of the darkness without losing yourself. You can't avoid or reframe suffering; it simply won't work.

At some point along your journey, you must realize that suffering is a part of life and you must make space for it. It can't be dealt with through mental reframing; it must be walked through. More than other types, it is easy to tell the difference between a SEVEN who has been through real suffering and has come out on the other side as the embodiment of sobriety and satisfaction, and the SEVEN who has yet to address pain and suffering. The SEVEN who has made space for suffering will still embody all of the fun aspects of SEVEN-ness but from a place of serenity and peace.

7

T Y P E

EIGHT

The Challenger / Protector / Advocate

An Enneagram EIGHT is also known as the Challenger, the Protector, or

the Advocate. They are strong, assertive, full of energy, honest, blunt, resourceful, and intense. They often have loud, powerful presences that are impossible to miss when they walk into a room. Because of these strong character traits, they are often assumed to be leaders and tend to assume leadership upon themselves. EIGHTs have a higher value for strong and competent authority than most other people have. When EIGHTs walk into a room, they immediately notice all of the social power dynamics. They can tell who carries influence, who thinks they're in charge but actually isn't, who is struggling to find their footing, and who feels like an outsider. EIGHTs have high values for justice, defending those who can't defend themselves and protecting themselves and others from corrupt or incompetent authority.

Having such clear superpowers doesn't come without a downside. Carrying so much strength and weight in everything they do leaves many EIGHTs quite hesitant to let anybody come close to them in the event that any real weaknesses are exposed and thus taken advantage of. EIGHTs can be masters of almost effortlessly keeping people away through their hard exterior, cutting words, and ability to see clearly what's going on underneath the surface. They have very sensitive radars for incompetence, untrustworthiness, or weakness in others. Because everybody has flaws and baggage of their own, EIGHTs sense the inadequacy of others and try to avoid being controlled by it all costs, often leaving them cynical, jaded, and isolated in the process. Seeing clearly isn't always the gift it's made out to be.

A World of EIGHTs

The world would be much more efficient with everyone thinking so straightforwardly all the time. Interactions would be easier because everyone would be completely honest and diplomatic. We would save hours and stress never having to wonder what others were thinking. Communication would be more candid, and conflict wouldn't last long. The world would be much more intense, for better or for worse, but it would also be less emotive and outwardly sensitive. Nothing would ever get done with everyone playing the role of queen bee, and nobody would trust anyone else's authority enough to let themselves be the worker bee. Chaos would ensue as people revolted against self-appointed authority.

Motivation

EIGHTs live under a compulsion to be strong and to come off as invincible. Autonomy is more important to EIGHTs than any other type, as they can always find reasons to not trust anybody in any situation. They do not want to be surprised or to be the ones personally paying the cost when the worst happens. Their knee-jerk response is to make sure that they and their loved ones are protected from harm. As a result, they become very resourceful, aggressive, and responsible people. Having a sturdy wall of defense around them at all times is their way of preventing anyone from taking advantage of them or being at the mercy of anyone but themselves. A common misconception is that EIGHTs always need to be in control, but their primary motivation is actually not wanting anyone else to control them in any way. Whether they impose their control on others is secondary to their vigilant desire to be free from the control of others.

The Shadow Side

In the pursuit of being loved, EIGHTs tend to settle for being respected or independent as the next best thing. It can be easy for an EIGHT to think that being seen as strong, having their authority and responsibility trusted, and having others get behind the decisions they make are about the best things that another person can do for them. Likewise, it can be easy for an EIGHT to mistake someone giving them space, not trying to control them, and letting them do what they want as the best form of love that there is. While all of these actions are usually good and usually meaningful for EIGHTs in particular, if they are the end rather than a means to the end, EIGHTs come up short of truly being known, honored, and celebrated for who they are.

These compulsions and subconscious motivations can lead to EIGHTs inadvertently building walls around themselves, which can take many forms: an aversion to any sort of vulnerability or known weaknesses, an inability to trust anyone, a need to be in control for their own safety, and the belief that the only way to live life is with a whole fortress of defenses.

The "deadly sin" or vice of EIGHTs is lust. While lust usually has sexual connotations, it shows up in a broader variety of ways for EIGHTs. It can be an insatiable desire for intensity, or the need to live their life at their desired volume and energy level. Most people in their average state do not meet an EIGHT's expected level of energy or relational stimulation. EIGHTs have enormous amounts of energy and feel emotions physically. This combination can lead to EIGHTs being restless and constantly unsatisfied with the mediocrity of life. An EIGHT's idea of fun can be a very heated argument or high-risk physical activities that get their adrenaline pumping. All of these factors can lead to EIGHTs easily steamrolling people, intimidating them, and generally communicating that others are beneath them or not worth their time if they don't meet their desired intensity.

EIGHTs in Integration and Disintegration

When EIGHTs are in stress or disintegration, they move toward the characteristics of FIVEs. Their general ability to be quick, bold, and decisive becomes more slow, reserved, and cautious. When they are usually forward-thinking and forward-moving, disintegration seemingly causes an EIGHT's activity to bottleneck and cease production. EIGHTs in disintegration can begin to simply absorb and hoard information without any particular outflow of what they're taking in. They can become stingy and possessive of their own time and energy. Whether it's in a  moment or a general season of life, EIGHTs who aren't doing well become fearful, paranoid, and secretive. It's worth noting that not all stress is automatically unhealthy or unhelpful for EIGHTs. Sometimes the high stakes of a situation can cause EIGHTs to slow down and prepare themselves more than they normally would, choosing to be as mentally prepared as possible rather

| OVERLY EMOTIONAL | MICROMANAGING | HOARDING ENERGY | FEARFUL |
| SECRETIVE | "FRIEND" OR "FOE" | SHORT FUSE | ISOLATING BEHAVIOR |

than relying on their gut instincts. When EIGHTs are doing well, they can use their movement toward FIVE to serve them rather than inhibit them.

When EIGHTs are healthy or integrated, they move toward the positive side of TWOs. They become generous with all of their time and energy and are more likely to extend others the benefit of the doubt. Healthy EIGHTs embrace emotional vulnerability, compassion, and empathy toward others. They're quicker to forgive and release people from disappointments that they've caused. Integrated EIGHTs can channel their strength and boldness toward the service of other people and help others flourish, rather than only being protected from harm. They will tear down seemingly impenetrable walls for the sake of people who need their help. Healthy EIGHTs are forces to be reckoned with, in the best way possible.

Digging Deeper into EIGHTs
ENNEADICTIONARY: HELPFUL EIGHT LANGUAGE

»— **Circles of Trust (n.):** EIGHTs are used to people not being able to handle their unfiltered selves. As a result, it often takes people much longer to earn an EIGHT's trust, because EIGHTs don't want to spend their energy on someone who will just be scared of them or dismiss them. EIGHTs will draw circles around their people and be very protective of them. There are layers to these circles of trust as well. An EIGHT will often only have one to three people that ever make it to the innermost circle.

»— **Intensity (n.):** EIGHTs naturally live their lives at a louder volume than most other people. They feel things deeply and have a lot of natural passion. While EIGHTs can definitely have strong anger, it's often their intensity that gets mistaken for anger, because most people are not as intense and passionate as EIGHTs are.

»→ **EIGHT Envy (n.):** Many people admire the strength, determination, powerful presence, and general coolness of EIGHTs. Some ONEs, THREEs, and SX SIXes claim to be EIGHTs because they see EIGHT strengths and weaknesses as more desirable than that of their own type. Other types have their own form of this occurrence, but EIGHTs who are even a little bit integrated can usually identify EIGHT envy in a second.

»→ **Confrontational Intimacy (n.):** EIGHTs fight as a way of making contact. Unaware EIGHTs don't understand how this kind of contact frightens others, nor do they notice that their blows go below the belt and are often hard to endure. They may delight in attacking, which they can perceive as "playful."

»→ **Hulk Mode (n.):** Most EIGHTs would probably tell you that they really don't like conflict, and they don't like "getting mad." What they do crave is intensity. When their own intense energy isn't matched by another person in a way they want it to be, EIGHTs have a way of escalating a situation to get the response they are looking for. Just like Bruce Banner/the Hulk, EIGHTs must acknowledge their own limitations; they are not invincible.

SUBTYPES

»→ **Self-Preservation (SP) EIGHT:** SP EIGHTs are highly practical and try to stay "close to home" in their circles of people as much as they can. They will rule over their small territory with an iron fist, and they want the walls around this territory to be impenetrable. The defensive gut impulses and occasional anger of SP EIGHTs can come out for seemingly smaller things like spam calls, noises that are a nuisance, outsiders who haven't been vetted, or someone not ordering enough food for the whole group. Like all EIGHTs, they are highly protective of their people, but SP EIGHTs are unlikely to flaunt all that they do.

»→ **Sexual (SX) EIGHT:** SX EIGHTs are the biggest personalities and are the most intense and high-energy of all EIGHTs. They're usually the people who are most likely to take charge and dive headfirst into unfamiliar situations, relying on their strong instincts to carry them through. They have the least patience for anything shallow or surface level, and they're more likely than the other EIGHT subtypes to intensify a situation just for the sake of intensity. SX EIGHTs quickly gravitate to leadership roles and embody the mentality of "you're either with me or against me." They place a high value on their close relationships, which they are very committed to.

Social (SO) EIGHT: SO EIGHTs are the countertype, meaning that they don't indulge in the lust for intensity in the same way that the other EIGHT subtypes do. They will often position themselves in the middle of a group or community of people and find a just cause to which they channel all of their influence and intensity. They are effective at rallying others to their side because of their commanding presence combined with their strong heart for others. SO EIGHTs also have their own way of creating enemies in addition to deeply loyal allies due to their ability to make strong waves in whole groups of people, for better or for worse.

WINGS

8W7   **8W9**

EIGHTs with a SEVEN wing (8w7) are highly energetic, assertive, and sharp minded. As a combination of two types in the Aggressive Stance, they are naturally very strong willed and can wield their words and their presence decisively. 8w7s are very active and have a seemingly endless capacity to do things. They have a stronger discomfort with tension or hard conversations than 8w9s do.

EIGHTs with a NINE wing (8w9) are often less outwardly intimidating than 8w7s are. They embody the "mama/papa bear" mentality in that they generally will not look to pick a fight or come after you unless they are provoked. They enjoy their comforts and keep to themselves more than 8w7s do. They are strong, stubborn, and very in touch with their gut feelings and intuitions. They live in constant tension between the need to assert themselves and rock the boat and the need to maintain peace and equilibrium.

TRIAD

EIGHTs are in the Body Triad, meaning they take in information intuitively through their bodies. When EIGHTs have strong emotions, they feel it physically more than types in the other triads do. EIGHTs have very strong gut reactions when they enter new situations and can rely on intuition. Each member of this triad has a unique relationship with anger as well. While ONEs outsource their anger and NINEs are asleep to their anger, EIGHTs swim in their anger. Some EIGHTs describe their anger like a river that's constantly coursing through their whole body. A path to health and integration for EIGHTs is learning how to channel their anger to productive action and justice.

STANCE

EIGHTs are in the Aggressive Stance, oriented against other people. For EIGHTs, this looks like a constant urge to keep people away and assert their own autonomy. People are untrustworthy until they are proven to be trustworthy. EIGHTs are strong, assertive, and know how to have their needs met, regardless of who may stand in the way. EIGHTs can struggle to understand the impact of their words and actions, as they often come off more strongly than they intend to. They draw clear boundaries around themselves and the people in their circles to keep unwanted people and activity away. Their orientation to time is the future, as they are always looking ahead for future plans and threats. They know where they want to go and what they want to do. All three types are also "feeling-repressed," meaning that they do and think more consciously than they feel. Fully processing or expressing feelings does not come naturally to EIGHTs. They're critical-thinking people of action who can think that feelings get in the way.

MISSED CONNECTIONS

Here are the "missed connections" for EIGHT:

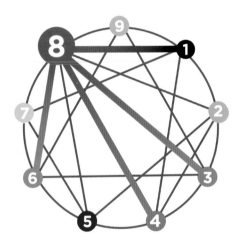

>→ **EIGHT and ONE:** ONEs and EIGHTs have a very strong sense of justice and ethics and will work hard to achieve them. They see things clearly. Both types will get very fiery when they don't perceive something to be right. Both types are argumentative and can be received as very intense people. They feel things physically, hate being manipulated, and experience anger very deeply.

>→ **EIGHT and THREE:** THREEs and EIGHTs are natural leaders, and you know when they walk into the room. Deep love for their people turns into action. They make great champions of people under their care. Both types hate inefficiency in all of its forms, inefficiency of feelings, and situations where people get emotional and don't come to solutions.

>→ **EIGHT and FOUR:** FOURs and EIGHTs have been told that they are "too much" their whole lives, perhaps because they are truly authentic. They are intense, feel very deeply, and are emotionally vulnerable, volatile, inspiring, and gracious. Neither type has any time at all for anything shallow or half-hearted. Both types can easily feel misunderstood or misrepresented.

»→ **EIGHT and SIX:** SIXes and EIGHTs are both strong protectors and guardians. Their deep loyalty to their people can ignite the flames of their fire. You really want both types to be *for* you, and you really don't want either type to be against you. They both have a hard time trusting authority and have a sharp eye for seeing trouble coming from a mile away.

If You Love an EIGHT

There's a good chance that there is at least one significant EIGHT in your life who you have loved for some time. Here are five things to bear in mind about how to best care for the EIGHTs in your life:

»→ **Don't try to quench their intensity.** The world is constantly telling EIGHTs that they're too much, too loud, need to calm down, and so on. The last people they need to hear that message from is their loved ones. This is especially true because those of us who are close to EIGHTs know how great it is to have someone with their energy and fearlessness on our side if we're ever in trouble or a situation gets heated. It is an immense disservice to EIGHTs if we only use their intensity when it's convenient for us. Sometimes they will feel strongly about something that you don't quite see or understand, and they need you to trust them. Sometimes their intensity is actually misdirected, but even in those situations, you can listen to them, work with them, help them reframe and redirect it, and rise to their level to help them see your point, among other things. Telling them to calm down will not usually help them or you.

»→ **Show up fully.** EIGHTs are either all in or all out; they don't do anything half-heartedly. They expect the same from people they love or respect. So, regardless of your EIGHT connection, it's important to understand that if you tell them that you'll do something, they expect your 100-percent effort. If they do something for you because they care, they will not be lazy about it or give a weak effort, so it honors EIGHTs to do the same for them.

»→ **Give them space to work things out.** Not many people like to be micromanaged, but EIGHTs especially do not like it. Autonomy is a huge value for them, and they don't want others to be asserting control over them. EIGHTs are strong, resilient, solution-oriented people, and they want to be respected as such. Most of the time they are good at solving problems and able to make decisions. Smothering or micromanaging an EIGHT will communicate to them that you don't trust them. Being given clear, reasonable expectations and a long leash communicates that you do trust them. They will recognize your efforts in extending trust to them, and it is appreciated.

8

»→ **If they go out of their way to give you advice, listen to it.** EIGHTs have strong protective instincts, and if you are in their circles, they care about you and want you to find success and competence. They usually don't involve themselves in the progress of others just because they feel like it. There is usually a reason, and it can be because they feel like they have something unique to offer your situation. They want you to be able to work through your problems and think critically. They want you to be able to take care of yourself. These desires come from values that are very important to EIGHTs for themselves, and they are acts that come very naturally to EIGHTs. If they try to help you out in these ways and you really take their advice to heart, it means the world to them.

»→ **Tell them when they're off.** When EIGHTs are on autopilot, their response to situations can often be "shoot first, ask questions later." Naturally, they will make mistakes and not see the error in their ways. One of the great things about EIGHTs is that they are usually able to take criticism objectively and then move on. You usually don't have to worry about what an EIGHT thinks of you, so try to return the favor. If they make you mad, you can say so without sugarcoating it. They prefer the honest truth. EIGHTs who are even a little bit healthy can take your criticism, and, most of the time, they will respect you for not cutting any corners or being afraid to rock the boat. They live life at a very loud volume, so sometimes they need to receive feedback at a loud volume as well.

The Way Forward
UNLEARN THE NESTING LIES

Every type has traps that they fall into when they are not aware of their internal narratives and motivations, and sometimes these can take the form of the lies that they believe about themselves and their place in the world around them. These lies end up becoming boxes that are built around us, and we need to hear and receive the truth that gets us out of these traps.

»→ **LIE: It is not okay to be weak or vulnerable.**
TRUTH: You are a human. You have weaknesses, and that is okay. Vulnerability can lead to tremendous growth and strength, and it helps others see and understand the real you.

NESTING LIES

It is not okay to be weak or vulnerable.

I can't trust anyone.

I need to be in control to feel safe.

Emotions are weakness.

I am too much.

8

»→ **LIE: I can't trust anyone.** TRUTH: Believe it or not, there are people out there who are both competent and have your best interests at heart. You have relational needs, and you were not meant to be the sole provider of everything. There are people who are ready to love you fiercely once you let them in.

»→ **LIE: I need to be in control to feel safe.** TRUTH: Not only are you not meant to always be the strongest, smartest, toughest, and most capable, but you *cannot* be all of those things either. It bears repeating that there are others who are also strong, capable, and care about you.

»→ **LIE: Emotions are weakness.** TRUTH: Your strength lies in your ability to express yourself honestly, clearly, and authentically. Emotions can be a gift both to you and to your loved ones.

»→ **LIE: I am too much.** TRUTH: You naturally have a lot of intensity and passion, and you were not made that way by mistake. When the world around you can't handle your strength, it is their loss, not yours.

RIPPLE EFFECTS

Your actions and tendencies have an influence on more people than just you, and it's better for everyone when you pay attention to this influence.

»→ When you are reluctant to be vulnerable or show any sign of weakness, what you're implicitly communicating to the people around you is that it's not okay to show any vulnerability and they have to act tough and strong at all times. You have a strong and influential presence, so when you act like it's not safe to open up or let down your defenses, the people around you notice and are likely to follow suit. When you present yourself as untouchable, people will be less likely to approach you. This ultimately cuts others off from the gifts you have and vice versa. In the process of trying to protect yourself and others, it is very possible that you still get hurt and cause hurt anyway.

»→ When you fan the flames to escalate tension for no reason other than being bored, it's not just others that pay the price. You become someone who can cause chaos very quickly for no apparent reason. It incentivizes others to walk on eggshells around you rather than being willing to meet you where you want to be met. You also solidify your own conceptions of people thinking that you're "too much" and unwilling to really engage with you. The whole act causes an unhealthy cycle of self-fulfilling prophecies where nobody wins. There are plenty of just and valid reasons to press into tension and raise your voice, but being bored is not one of them. When you wield this power for no reason other than because you can, it reduces the impact when this power actually needs to be used.

»→ Remember that you often carry more influence than you realize. When you aggressively push for your own agenda in any given situation, you take up enough space that it affects the experience others are having. You don't even have to be trying to seize control of whatever the situation is. Your agenda could simply be "get me out of here" in a situation where you don't trust the authority, but it still inhibits the people close to you. In these cases, you're preventing others from engaging without providing any sort of alternate solution. It even limits those under your care whom you want to protect, because you're not letting them form their own opinions about who or what is trustworthy. *You* then become the only trusted authority for them. There are some situations where pushing your own agenda may be appropriate, but it always causes broader ripple effects than you might think.

SELF-CARE FOR EIGHTS

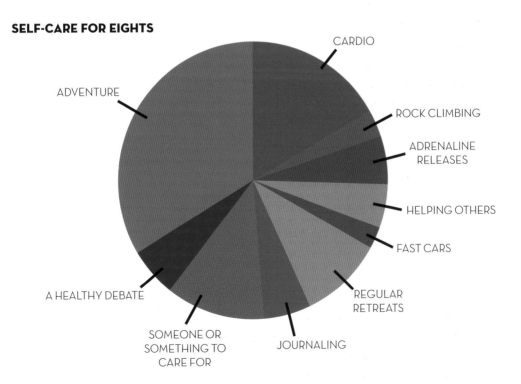

BODY

| OVER-EXTENDING/
POSSIBLY VIOLENT | COMBATIVE/ RECKLESS | ACTIVE/DRIVEN FROM WITHIN |

MIND

| HARD-HEADED/ MEGALOMANIA | PROUD/ IMPOSING
SELF ON OTHERS | COURAGEOUS/DECISIVE |

HEART

| IMMORAL "CON ARTIST" | DENYING OWN EMOTIONAL
NEEDS | SELF-SURRENDER TO
HIGHER POWER |

SELF

| DELUSIONS OF POWER +
INVINCIBILITY | BOASTFUL/EGOCENTRIC | SELF-CONFIDENT/SELF-ASSERTIVE |

OTHERS

| RUTHLESS/DICTATORIAL | DOMINATING/NOT INCLUSIVE | GENEROUS/PROTECTIVE |

JUST FOR FUN!

| THE HULK | IRON MAN | WONDER WOMAN |

HEALTHY PRACTICES

»→ **Compassion.** EIGHTs are filled with compassion for the underdog. It's not enough for you to speak out against injustice; you have to get your hands dirty. You feel the need to get involved, to stand in the shoes of those you're trying to help. You have a great capacity for empathy. Showing compassion by stepping in and physically serving the underprivileged is a way of living into your true self.

➤ **Accountability.** EIGHTs tend to avoid vulnerability and letting others get close out of fear of being controlled by them. To overcome your insecurity, you need accountability from people you know you can trust. You need a context where you can be known and where you can be weak. If not, you will spend your life hiding your true self behind an image of power.

➤ **Space for Expression.** You often feel like you need to tone your whole self down because others don't know how to respond to you. You have more energy than any other type and can pick fights or accelerate situations because you're bored and want to see some action. A really important practice for your health is to have a safe place to live at full volume. Whether this is physically exerting energy, being with people with whom you can be as unfiltered as you want, or a creative outlet, you need a place where you don't need to worry about toning it down.

The Reckoning

Many people need some sort of intense clash or conflict with their normal MO to be freed from unhealthy compulsive patterns. We describe this reckoning for EIGHTS as "tenderizing." When you think of meat becoming tenderized, it involves being hit repeatedly and forcefully with a heavy object to give it a more favorable texture. The more an EIGHT builds up their own fortress to keep people away, the louder, harder, and heavier the force will have to be in order to break through to the actual soul behind the tough exterior. Some blows are too painful for even the most brash EIGHT to ignore, and sometimes that is what it takes for an EIGHT on autopilot to actually nurture themselves and grow beyond the walls they build to keep people out.

The path to freedom comes in the form of tenderness and rediscovering innocence. The good news for EIGHTS is that you get to choose whether you find that through the violent tenderizing process, or through small, gradual, conscious, and willing steps toward the innocence that you never had. While the latter path is ultimately less painful in the long run, we recognize that it's still going to be hard and scary. It involves letting fallible people in a little bit closer. It means that you might be under someone else's control for a time. Lowering your defenses, by definition, involves exposing potential weaknesses. It involves trusting people who are capable of letting you down. A step toward innocence is a step away from cynicism. A step toward vulnerability is a step away from being completely surrounded by your walls. It's in this innocence that you will find your truest strength. Mature EIGHTs can access tenderness, innocence, and gentleness with ease, because they have learned to control their own strength, rather than letting their strength control them. The impact of this sort of tenderness can be truly transformative both for you and all of the communities to which you belong.

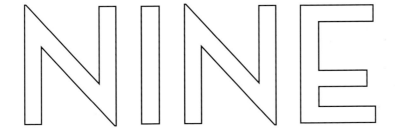

T Y P E
NINE

The Peacemaker / Mediator / Reconciler

Enneagram NINEs

Enneagram NINEs are also known as peacemakers, mediators, or reconcilers. They are easygoing, patient, agreeable, steady, relaxed, and comforting. They also have a surprisingly fiery side that doesn't come out every day. NINEs are people who have a strong bent toward peace and harmony. They can sense any tension when they walk into a room and are gifted at both staying away from it or resolving it, depending on their circumstances. They are truly gifted at seeing and understanding both sides to every story, making all sorts of people feel welcomed and heard. In movies, NINEs are the people who either mentally or physically check out whenever the tension escalates. They feel and take on the stress of other people. NINEs are similar to hobbits from Tolkien's *The Lord of the Rings* series in that they really are content with peace, quiet, good food, and the simple pleasures of life. They're usually not particularly looking for a big adventure. A chief desire for NINEs is to avoid being inconvenienced or interrupted by life.

The peace that NINEs reflect on the outside is not always indicative of what's going on inside. In their constant evasion of conflict or tension, they inadvertently suppress any sort of negative thought or emotion that requires too much energy to deal with. The longer they avoid all things negative, the more they become like a volcano waiting to erupt. They end up getting stuck in all sorts of unpleasant situations they'd rather not be in because of the effort required in asserting themselves and rocking the boat. Seeing every perspective so clearly leads to all sorts of indecision and internal conflict because they're so used to living in the grey.

A World of NINEs

The world would be quieter, less intense, and less polarized. There would never be war, as no one would start any fights, and everyone would defer to everyone else. People would constantly be apologizing, often for things that never happened, and everyone would be better at listening to all sides. Everyone would lovingly accept everything, and the world would be agreeable and peaceful on the surface. However, under the surface, everyone would be boiling with passive-aggression and pent-up rage. No one would ever say what they really mean, nothing would be punctual, and nothing would ever get done because no one could decide what to do.

Motivation

The desire for peace and calm that NINEs experience is actually a constant compulsion to be in harmony with the world around them. Their knee-jerk response is to always choose the path of least resistance, and they often find themselves with less energy to deal with the troubles of life than other types. NINEs strive to be able to do whatever they please. They don't want to cause trouble or be troubled. NINEs are often, but not always, people who are prone to having hundreds of unread texts and emails. When they work through items on to-do lists, unaware NINEs will work through them in order of convenience rather than importance. They don't like to be hurried, often leading to slow and meandering speech and activity. These patterns are greatly due to a NINE's belief that they don't actually have enough energy, resources, or stamina to deal with the problems that they face. Their subconscious defense mechanism becomes evading tension and finding whatever semblance of peace and harmony they can, regardless of what's happening below the surface.

The Shadow Side

For a multitude of reasons, when NINEs truly seek love, acceptance, and understanding, they subconsciously end up settling for a ceasefire instead of true love and belonging. Whether it's because they don't believe that they're truly worthy, because of the great effort required to deal with what's below the surface, because of a lack of energy, or because of their ability to be content very easily, NINEs can settle for the next-best thing. You could even say that they settle for settling itself. The sort of "above the surface only" peace that unaware NINEs gravitate toward is a cheapened version of the real thing, but it's what they pursue because it requires less energy. Seeking to understand and uproot whatever unhealthy habits and ideas lie below the surface is a scary pursuit to NINEs, full of unknowns and challenges. They see this pursuit as walking through a field full of land mines, so they gravitate to staying put and believing that if nothing is blowing up, then everyone is okay.

NINEs tell themselves plenty of narratives that aren't actually true, yet they still hold a lot of power in their lives. These narratives include but are not limited to the belief that their voice and presence doesn't matter, that it's not okay to impose their will on anyone or anything, that they have to roll with the punches or else they're being selfish, that they don't have what it takes to make hard decisions, that they need to keep peace more than they need to pay attention to their own needs, and that nobody actually notices or cares about them. Early on in their lives, NINEs learn how to evade and dissolve conflict as a survival strategy to the point that it becomes their primary MO. Consequently, everyone around them gets used to them being neutral, agreeable presences who will affirm and validate them, regardless of how right or wrong they are. We learn to take NINEs for granted, and they internalize what we implicitly communicate to them.

Wrapped up in all of these complicated motivations and behaviors is the core vice or "deadly sin" for NINEs, which is sloth. Sloth can come in the form of physical laziness, when menial tasks pile up and up because NINEs lack the energy and/or assertiveness to get on top of them, when they don't leave their cozy sanctuaries for hours or days on end, or when they let their external worlds become cluttered and disorganized. However, it generally refers to a more internal slothfulness, lack of initiative, and unwillingness to expend energy. Their slothfulness can show up in social laziness, when they don't go out of their way to see or talk to people if they don't have to. It can show up in interpersonal laziness, when they don't want to deal with conflict because of the great amount of energy and discomfort that would be required. It can show up in professional or situational laziness, when they get far too comfortable with the mediocre or subpar status quo, because staying is easier than shaking things up. When NINEs are not aware of their tendencies, sloth dictates much of their action (or lack thereof). Sloth is also a defense mechanism of sorts, where NINEs try to protect themselves from feeling incapable of dealing with any real hardships or problems.

NINEs in Integration and Disintegration

When NINEs are in seasons or moments of disintegration or stress, they take on some characteristics of SIXes. Their usual calm and relaxed demeanor can become paranoid, anxious, and defensive. Their minds race with constant thoughts and fears rather than taking things slowly as they usually do. The default response of NINEs to tension or relational blips is to smooth things out, extend the benefit of the doubt, or to generally ignore any negative feelings that may arise in them. In instantaneous moments of stress or general pat-

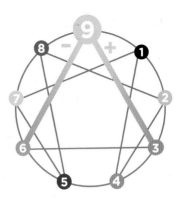

terns of disintegration, NINEs become quicker to assume the worst and internally escalate the tension beyond what the situation calls for. Their general subconscious belief that their presence doesn't matter rises to the surface and becomes much louder in their minds and in their actions. NINEs taking on attributes of SIXes isn't necessarily an unhealthy movement. When life's circumstances become more stressful or have higher stakes for NINEs, they can channel SIX characteristics in a way that serves them. Sometimes there are situations that require more anticipation of what could go wrong and subsequent planning around those scenarios. If a NINE is encountering a significant project, assignment, or other life event that increases stress, the SIX qualities of having a racing mind, scanning for potential threats, and general unease can keep a NINE sharp and alert. Not all stress is indicative of disintegration.

WARNING SIGNS

ANALYSIS PARALYSIS/
OVERTHINKING

EASILY AGITATED

PICKING FIGHTS

PARANOIA

NARCOTIZING

NUMBING

WITHDRAWING

WORST-CASE-
SCENARIO THINKING

Healthy, integrated NINEs move toward the positive side of THREEs. Their general pattern of withdrawing and dulling their desires becomes much more proactive. When NINEs are doing well, their minds are sharp, decisive, and lead quickly to action. They understand that they have value, they have something to contribute, and their voice is worthy of being heard. They can clearly see the harmony that they desire and the steps needed to get there, so they become much more willing and ready to assert themselves for the sake of peace. NINEs on autopilot often feel asleep to much of the world around them in their desire to be unbothered by life, but when they move toward THREE in health, they are highly engaged with their surroundings and their own internal agency. The slothfulness that they usually struggle with turns into activity, accomplishment, and finding their own voice.

Digging Deeper into NINEs

ENNEADICTIONARY: HELPFUL NINE LANGUAGE

»→ **Merging (v.):** NINEs have a tendency to merge or become one with others, meaning they may find that they agreed or aligned with someone for the sake of peace when in fact they do not agree with this person. It can also look like agreeing to do an activity that they don't want to do or doing an activity the same way someone else does rather than how they'd do it by themselves.

»→ **Inner Sanctum (n.):** All of life is exhausting for a NINE who is trying to maintain external and internal peace at all times, so they can be known to take little vacations into their minds, or inner sanctum.

»→ **One-Hundred-Mile Stare (n.):** NINEs sometimes give the impression of being absent-minded or slightly befuddled. If nothing is happening around them, they will check out. They can even suddenly fall asleep in broad daylight. The one-hundred-mile stare is when a NINE checks out mid-conversation.

»→ **Numbing/Narcotizing (v.):** The defense mechanism of NINEs is to numb or narcotize through anything from watching videos online to staring into space to food, exercise, or something more dangerous like drugs. Because they don't feel adequate to the many challenges of life, they may take refuge in some sort of addiction. NINEs seek these stimulants and strong sensations from outside because they can find it difficult to stimulate themselves.

SUBTYPES

»→ **Self-Preservation (SP) NINE:** SP NINEs are more inclined toward routines than the other NINE subtypes. They love very tangible things that bring them comfort, whether that be eating, sleeping, exercise, or reading. The stereotype of NINEs wanting to live entirely within their cozy little worlds with lots of warm laughter, good food, peace, and quiet is most descriptive of SP NINEs. SP NINEs find comfort in their routines because routines are their way of engaging with life in a predictable manner, minimizing the energy that new challenges require. SP NINEs can become frustrated and irritable when their rhythms are interrupted and thus need to expend their energy on unwanted challenges.

»→ **Sexual (SX) NINE:** SX NINEs crave intensity and adventure and are more excitable than the other NINE subtypes. They are also more prone toward merging, and they do so deeply with a handful of close relationships. SX NINEs can feel, explore, and live vicariously through these significant relationships in their lives and have a harder time being alone. They can easily vacillate between feeling wild and adventurous and wanting to retreat back inside of their shells. While SP NINEs can lose themselves in their routines, SX NINEs can lose themselves in close relationships.

»→ **Social (SO) NINE:** Many SO NINEs do not present like other NINEs at all because of their inclination toward whole groups of people. They can come across as SEVEN-ish as people see them as lighthearted and easy to float around social groups. SO NINEs can gravitate toward central roles in groups for the sake of mediating or bringing people together, forgetting themselves in the process. They are the countertype, meaning they don't approach slothfulness the same way that SX and SP NINEs do. Rather than letting slothfulness overtake them physically, they suppress and avoid internal problems by busying themselves physically and socially. They act as if bringing peace and harmony to the people around them will somehow bring it to their internal worlds as well.

9

WINGS

9W8   9W1

NINEs with an EIGHT wing (9w8) live in a constant tension between a desire to keep the peace and a desire to rock the boat about whatever injustice they're facing. They can feel at times as if they are two different people that go back and forth between who's controlling their words and actions. 9w8s are generally more assertive, outwardly passionate, and anti-authoritarian than 9w1s.

NINEs with a ONE wing (9w1) also live in constant tension between the desire to be unbothered by life and a desire to right all of the wrongs that they encounter, which inevitably requires action and inconveniencing themselves. They are generally more inwardly focused, idealistic, orderly, and dutiful than 9w8s. 9w1s generally have some sort of outlet for their organizing. Their "go with the flow" personalities often have a couple areas where they are more rigid and structured.

TRIAD

NINEs are in the Body Triad, meaning they take in information intuitively through their bodies. Their first reaction, even if it's instantaneous, is a physical one. They have strong gut feelings about what to do, even if they don't always act on it. NINEs also feel emotions physically, especially all of the tension that they place on themselves. Anger is a primary motivating factor for all three types in the triad. NINEs are asleep to their anger. They often ignore or suppress their anger because they feel that it would take less energy to suppress it than act on it. NINEs fall asleep to their anger subconsciously most of the time, which can look like realizing that they're angry minutes, hours, or even days after the event that triggers their anger. Sometimes, NINEs realize that they're angry when they feel it somewhere in their bodies.

STANCE

NINEs are in the Withdrawing Stance. They are oriented away from other people, with a strong tendency to retreat inwardly. NINEs live much of their lives in their own internal worlds. They can easily get lost in their own thoughts, live entire scenarios in their imaginations, and even settle or resolve conflict with others without actually communicating with them. NINEs also withdraw to preserve their own sense of autonomy if anyone tries too hard to force them into anything. All three types in the Withdrawing Stance are doing-repressed, meaning that they think and feel more intuitively than they "do" or act. They often have deep, brilliant, sensitive minds, and their primary struggle is actually involving themselves and imposing their will on the environment around them. Even though NINEs are in the Body Triad, they are still doing-repressed. They have physical, gut responses to situations, but their default next step is to suppress rather than to move into action.

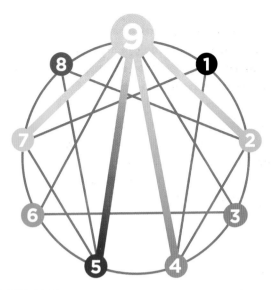

Here are the "missed connections" for NINE:

»⟶ **NINE and TWO:** TWOs and NINEs are both self-forgetting types. While NINEs merge to keep the peace (and to be left alone), thereby forgetting themselves, TWOs hide behind others with more dominant personalities in order to find value in themselves and their relationships. Both types are empathetic, generous, serving types and may struggle with saying no. They each have their own way of feeling other people's feelings.

»⟶ **NINE and FOUR:** FOURs and NINEs can identify with a sense of not fully belonging. As such, they may bend toward self-absorption and can come across as dramatic. As members of the Withdrawing Stance, they are oriented toward the past, which comes across as nostalgic. Both types also love stories, especially fantasy/fiction that allows them to escape into other worlds.

»⟶ **NINE and FIVE:** FIVEs and NINEs are both in the Withdrawing Stance and have strong avoidant tendencies. They are private and reserved. They are good listeners, hold the secrets of others, and create cognitive distance to stay safe. Both types are perceptive, deep thinkers who enjoy intellectually stimulating conversations and topics. Both types also value sleep *a lot*.

»⟶ **NINE and SEVEN:** SEVENs and NINEs don't look like they have a lot in common on the surface, but both types are extremely pain avoidant. They are both fun-loving, generous, versatile, and adaptable types, ready to go with the flow. Both types can also come across as distractible or scattered.

If You Love a NINE

There's a good chance that there is at least one significant NINE in your life who you have loved for some time. Here are five things to bear in mind about how to best care for the NINEs in your life:

»→ **Don't interrupt them.** A constant struggle for NINEs is feeling like their voice and presence doesn't matter, so they are often hesitant to insert their opinions or take up any sort of significant space at all. When you interrupt them or talk over them, the implicit message that you communicate is that what you have to say is more important than what they have to say and that their voice is less important. All of us would do well to listen to NINEs, as they are gifted at hearing both sides and helping us consider perspectives that we wouldn't normally consider. We all lose when we talk over NINEs and don't listen to what they have to say. Don't discourage them from taking up space.

»→ **Make space for them to assert their voice.** NINEs are hesitant to express unpopular opinions or to rock the boat in any way. If you're close to a NINE, it may be easier for you to tell if they're upset or frustrated than it is for everybody else. It's never their inclination to draw any sort of attention to themselves, even if *you* know that they have something important to say. Sometimes there will be situations that call for you to advocate for them and say whatever it is that they're not willing to say themselves, but very often the best thing for them is to be able to use their own voice. If they're trying to say something and others aren't hearing them, draw attention to your NINE. If they're feeling hesitant to say something, validate and encourage them. If they know what they want to say but don't know how to say it, be their sounding board and help them think through when to speak up. Making space for NINEs will not only make them feel validated and important, but it is crucial for their own growth and development as well.

»→ **If you have conflict that involves them, be patient and persistent.** As we've discussed earlier in this chapter, NINEs don't love conflict. Yet conflict handled with grace and maturity is crucial to helping all of us, including NINEs, grow beyond our current limitations. Even if the NINEs in your life want to avoid the conflict that involves them, it is beneficial to everyone for it to be addressed. NINEs generally gravitate toward the path of least resistance, and conflict involves resistance. If you think they're mad at you, you may have to be very persistent if you want them to open up. When they do open up, take them seriously. If they don't say anything right away, stick around. Sometimes it can take them a very long time to come to terms with their own feelings about conflict. Remember that they don't respond to tension the same way that you do, so looking at it through their perspective will help you both move toward resolution.

»→ **Treat them like a priority.** NINEs subconsciously don't act like they are a priority to anyone, nor do their internal narratives tell them that they are a priority. They are highly accommodating people who will go out of their way to make sure that people around them aren't inconvenienced. If the rest of us aren't conscious about our actions or relationships, it can be extremely easy to thoughtlessly talk over NINEs, walk all over them, and take them for granted. Show your love to a NINE by making it loud and clear that they're a priority in your life, that they're worth being inconvenienced over, that you notice what they say and do, and that you want to have them around you. They're not quick to prioritize themselves, so there will be times when they need you to help them out.

The Way Forward
UNLEARN THE NESTING LIES

Every type has traps that they fall into when they are not aware of their internal narratives and motivations, and sometimes these can take the form of the lies that they believe about themselves and their place in the world around them. These lies end up becoming boxes that are built around us, and we need to hear and receive the truth that gets us out of these traps.

»→ **LIE: It's not okay to assert myself.** TRUTH: Not only is it okay to assert yourself because you have just as much of a right to as everybody else in the world, but it's likely that others will notice if it's not something you normally do. Healthy people who love and respect you will honor the instances when you do assert yourself.

»→ **LIE: My wants and needs don't matter.** TRUTH: They matter just as much as everybody else's do. You are no less worthy than all of the people whose wants and needs you place value on.

»→ **LIE: Keeping the peace is more important than I am.** TRUTH: "Peace" that results in a ceasefire but leaves you unresolved, unheard, and unsatisfied isn't actually peace. It simply redirects the tension or chaos rather than resolving it. Your own internal sense of peace is an essential part of the equation.

»→ **LIE: Nobody sees or understands me.** TRUTH: People want to hear your voice and enjoy your presence much, much more than you realize. You bring peace and stability that people long for.

»→ **LIE: I'm not special.** TRUTH: The weight that you carry is remarkable, and that comes with seeing peace and harmony with more clarity than most people do. Your ability to empathize is truly a gift, and your internal fire is always a pleasant surprise.

RIPPLE EFFECTS

Your actions and tendencies have an influence on more people than just you, and it's better for everyone when you pay attention to this influence.

»→ Avoiding conflict generally isn't a good habit, but it's more than just you who pays the price of your avoidance. While there are certainly situations where conflict eventually dissolves with time, frequently the situation can get worse the longer that problems go unaddressed. Avoiding small problems will only make it more of your default response to ignore bigger problems. Conflict almost always has at least one other party as well. If you leave tension unaddressed with one or more other people, it leaves them nothing but space to fill in all of the gaps about you, your intentions, what you think about them, and so on. When you don't insert your own voice, opinions, and presence into situations of conflict, your relationships often end up worse than they were before. Internally resolving conflict on your own doesn't mean that the conflict has actually gotten resolved with the other party.

»→ Many NINEs are great at appearing to be content in almost any situation and not complaining about anything. This is a wonderful quality. However, it can be challenging for the rest of us to determine whether you are *actually* content or if you're just merging, avoiding, or suppressing in order to not make a scene. If you don't give even the slightest clue as to what you actually want or what's actually bothering you, then it leaves the people close to you guessing, feeling frustrated, and wondering if you actually care. If people ask you what you want or what you think, they generally actually want to know your answer. People close to you are probably way more willing to accommodate your desires than you give them credit for. Sometimes your desire to not rock the boat actually causes more relational strain than if you were to state your unpopular opinion.

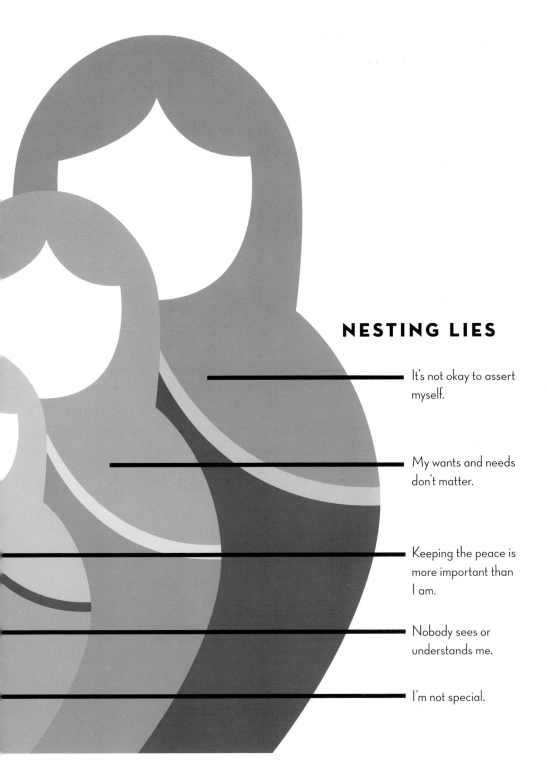

NESTING LIES

It's not okay to assert myself.

My wants and needs don't matter.

Keeping the peace is more important than I am.

Nobody sees or understands me.

I'm not special.

9

»→ We know that you often feel like your presence and voice don't actually matter. When you delete yourself from the equation and live as if this were true, people notice and respond accordingly. Sometimes they will chase you harder than you want to be chased. Sometimes they will begin to believe things about you that aren't actually true. Sometimes they'll be hurt by your relational absence. Sometimes they will simply move on and act as if you're not there because you're not willing to show up. The whole process starts a very dangerous cycle that only further reinforces your own belief. The people around you need you to show up, and you need it yourself too. When you delete yourself from the equation, everyone else involved naturally and obviously loses something important.

NINEs want to be taken care of, don't want to be rushed or pressured, and want to be taken seriously. They need you to listen to them, walk with them through hardships, and to be reminded that even if you're in conflict with them, you still love them and they'll still be okay.

HEALTHY PRACTICES

»→ **Surrender.** NINEs will find the practice of surrender challenging. Surrender is the discipline that frees us to let go of the burden of always needing to get our own way. NINEs are often unaware of all the anger and tension that they are holding on to, so the practice of naming and releasing these burdens will help NINEs truly find this peace.

»→ **Nature Walks.** Walking trails, hiking, climbing, biking, jogging, or strolling the park or beach aid the NINE in restoring balance and return them to a sense of peace and calm. Nature reminds them that, though we live in a world of chaos, there is a natural order to life. You can be reminded of how the world is much bigger than you and what's currently troubling you, and it always has been.

»→ **Peacemaking.** NINEs shouldn't feel bad about their desire to help others resolve conflict. Look for ways to use this gift. It's a stretching practice for you because you have to enter in and involve yourself in the messiness of relationships, but it's one of the most natural ways you can serve others around you.

»→ **Acknowledging Needs and Desires.** Everyone has needs and everyone has desires. An important step toward NINEs finding their own voice is identifying and claiming their needs. It can be as simple as writing down two or three simple needs or desires in your journal every day, but it's crucial for your growth that you make space to figure out what you want and what you need.

SELF-CARE FOR NINES

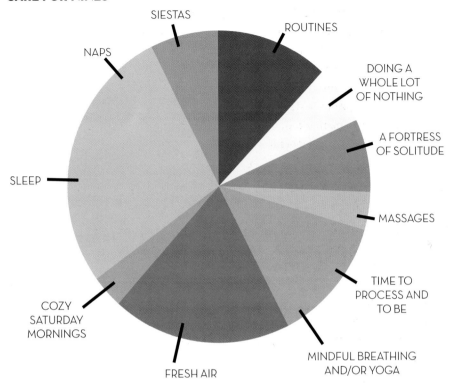

SIESTAS

NAPS

ROUTINES

DOING A
WHOLE LOT
OF NOTHING

A FORTRESS
OF SOLITUDE

SLEEP

MASSAGES

TIME TO
PROCESS AND
TO BE

COZY
SATURDAY
MORNINGS

MINDFUL BREATHING
AND/OR YOGA

FRESH AIR

9

BODY

CATATONIC/NEGLECTFUL   ACTIVE YET DISENGAGED   ACTIVE YET DISENGAGED

MIND

OBSTINATE/NUMB   HAZY THINKING/INATTENTIVE   OPTIMISTIC

HEART

REPRESSED/NEGLECTFUL   INDIFFERENT/INDOLENT   EMOTIONALLY STABLE/SERENE

SELF

ABANDONING OF SELF   SPEAK IN PHILOSOPHY + STOCK   AUTONOMOUS/TRUSTING
                            SAYINGS RATHER THAN TRUE SELF   OF SELF

OTHERS

BLOCKING PEOPLE OUT   IDEALIZING OTHERS/DOING THEIR   HARMONIZING IN GROUPS
                                      WISHES

IN CONFLICT

DISASSOCIATING FROM   ACCOMMODATING/   MEDIATING/SYNTHESIZING
CONFLICT   "PEACE AT ANY PRICE"

The Reckoning

When NINEs don't address their unhealthy patterns and habits, they can end up evading and avoiding all sorts of difficulties and problems to the point that it spirals downward into isolation, depression, and broken relationships. It can take the extreme version of many of these experiences to awaken NINEs from their sleepwalking through life. Sometimes the reckoning will come in the form of a conflict that is too great to ignore, or carrying so much unresolved tension that it breaks you in multiple ways. It can take extreme circumstances to break NINEs of the compulsion to suppress problems. It can take dramatic events to free you from the inability to speak up and rock the boat.

NINEs are daily faced with choices to continue in their unaware spirals or to step away from them toward decisive action. NINEs can learn these lessons the slow, gradual way or the painful, dramatic way. The former often involves seeing resistance and moving toward it anyway. It involves looking deep within yourself and your relationships and other circumstances to find and uproot the patterns that hold them back. It involves breaking up some hard ground for the sake of planting something new. It involves looking far into the horizon and choosing *that* peace rather than the more instantaneous peace. NINEs have opportunities to take decisive action in small, simple ways every day. The more you choose this more difficult pursuit, the more you'll find yourself able to resolve, mediate, and reconcile bigger and bigger problems. You'll become the very peace that you seek. The path to growth brings true harmony not only to them but also to the world around them. NINEs have the daily opportunity to have their deepest desire become their greatest gift to the world.

9

The Way Forward

● ● ● ● ● ● ● ● ●

The Enneagram has a beautiful and painful way of exposing us. Many times when someone discovers their Enneatype, they experience a lot of anger, shame, or annoyance that their deepest motivations and core vices have been named. So what now? You know your Enneatype, you've learned some new language, and you've heard some challenges for growth. What's next?

»→ **Don't let the Enneagram be an excuse for your bad behavior.** We hope that you have uncovered some of the lies you have been believing, some of the bad habits you have fallen prey to, or some of the unhealthy narratives you have been telling yourself. Your work now is to combat those lies with truth, to unlearn bad habits, and to rewrite your unhealthy narratives. Do not use the Enneagram as an excuse to continue in bad habits and hurtful behavior. Now that you know better, do better.

»→ **Don't become enslaved to your type.** This is just one facet of who you are and how you show up in the world. The Enneagram will never tell you everything about who you are. While it is incredibly helpful, it is not everything.

»→ **Don't type other people.** If you're interested in learning about those around you, spend some time and dig deep into all nine types. This will help you better understand the different ways that people view the world. Stop short of projecting those types onto your loved ones. No one likes that.

»→ **Don't force the Enneagram onto other people.** It is not the only way to gain self-awareness and personal growth. It's not a tool that resonates with everyone, and that's okay.

»—→ **Ask for help.** You may have uncovered some hard truths in this book that you need to unpack with a professional. Please do that! Find a counselor, mental health professional, spiritual director, or other experienced advocate who can help walk with you on this journey. We all need help, and we're in this together.

»—→ **Don't be hard on yourself when autopilot kicks in.** Even if you think you have already "done your work" with the Enneagram, when the storms of life roll in, it is all too easy to fall back into old habits or find yourself in a season of disintegration. Give yourself grace. This is a journey, and it will have its ups and downs.

In the end, remember that self-knowledge is not an end in itself; rather, it is an invitation to grow. No matter what you do with this new knowledge, we hope it is for good and for growth. You now have more language and understanding for how we work as humans. Use this for compassion and empathy. Use this to build people up and to see those around you with new eyes.

We hope you enjoyed this book as much as we enjoyed writing it. Thank you for trusting us with your time. Feel free to reach out to us on Instagram with your questions and comments @justmyenneatype.

Your friends,
Josh and Liz

Acknowledgments

• • • • • • • • •

First and foremost, we have to thank the "Brain Trust" group chat of Jamie, Hilary, Rachel, and Will. Thanks for being a constantly fun and insightful crew with whom we could get into the Enneagram. You have helped the Enneagram become a process of mutual discovery for all of us, and we are always learning more and more about ourselves and about the world from each of you. Thank you for being incredible friends who have been with Josh in this process from the very beginning and for opening up your lives to include Liz.

To all of our Eastbrook friends who showed up week after week to support us as we taught our first class: Mac, Ethan, Lisa, Audrey, Liz, Zack, Gabe, Eric, Isabelle, Jewel, Jessie, Erik, Kristen, and Joanna, and to Eastbrook for giving us a platform to teach. All of your support from the very beginning helped make our Instagram account—and then this book—possible.

To the whole team at Quarto, particularly Amanda, Marissa, Jessi, and Lydia. Thank you so much for reaching out to us, entrusting us with this platform, and making a way for us to reach a wider audience.

To Josh's family. To my parents Tim and Ellen, brother Jamie, sister JoJo, to Aunt Judy and Uncle Andy, and cousins Stephen, Amy, Ben, Alyssa, Joey, Grace, Isaac, Rachel, Emma, and Maddie—thank you all for being my biggest fans, always checking in on me through every step of the writing process, and shaping me to be who I am now. Your countless means of support have had an immense influence.

To Liz's family. My parents, Ruth and Nick, have always supported every new passion project and endeavor of mine, and this book has been no exception. Everyone deserves parents who are champions like they are. To Andrea and Tyler, for your ongoing support and for always feeding me. To Saige, Harrison, and Lorelai, who bring me more joy than I could ever put into words. To my framily for supporting me daily: Becky, Lisa, Audrey, Jill, Leah, Jessie, and Hannah.

To Camille and Brandon, who introduced us to the Enneagram. Thank you, Camille, for showing a young, scattered, and overextended TWO that slowing down and becoming self-aware is about the most others-serving thing one can possibly do. Thank you, Brandon, for the way you name profound truths in innovative ways and always challenge and inspire this FIVE. Your deeply rooted knowledge of the Enneagram and wisdom have changed our lives. Thank you.

To everyone who helped contribute to these chapters. To the ONEs—Hil, Zack, and Erica; the TWOs—Alice and Jazzy; the THREEs—Will and Kristen; the FOURs—Chris, Mac, and Alyssa; Kristen—the FIVE; the SIXes—Aunt Judy, Jamie, and Rachel; The SEVENs—Brandon, Rachel, Liz, and Nic; The EIGHTs—Luke and Isaac; and Jamie—the NINE. Thank you for giving us deeper understanding and more precise language. Our writing is more clear, cohesive, and insightful because of your time and generosity, so thank you.

To the Enneagram teachers who have gone before us. In particular, Richard Rohr, Beatrice Chestnut, and Chris Heuertz. There are so many more we could name, and we are daily humbled to play a small role in the Enneagram's unfolding in the world. We hope we have done it justice and taught with great care.

Lastly, to everyone who follows us over at @justmyenneatype on Instagram. It never ceases to amaze us how many of you appreciate, internalize, and advocate for our work, show us support, send encouraging messages, give new ideas, and do the hard work required for growth. Thank you for supporting us and sticking with us because this book would not be a reality if it weren't for you all.

About the Authors

• • • • • • • • •

Liz Carver and **Josh Green** run one of the most popular Enneagram accounts on social media, **@justmyenneatype** (justmyenneatype.com). Liz is a designer and the director of communication at Eastbrook Church in Wisconsin, and Josh is a campus minister for InterVarsity Christian Fellowship.

Index

● ● ● ● ● ● ● ● ●